The Constant Traveller

When the journey is all that matters

The fourth book in the 'Simple Life' series

by Mary-Jane Houlton

Other books by Mary-Jane Houlton

'Simple Life' series

Just Passing Through (Book 1)

A Simple Life (Book 2)

The Turning of the Seasons (Book 3)

Other books

How to be a House-Sitter

Contents

Introduction 9

Part 1 – The lost years **13**

Chapter 1: Living through a pandemic on a boat 15

Chapter 2: Finding a new equilibrium 24

Chapter 3: The lost years 2020–2021 32

Chapter 4: House-sitting – a new way to travel 38

Part 2 – A new beginning **51**

Chapter 5: The journey begins again 53

Chapter 6: The Nivernais – finding paradise 62

Chapter 7: Dancing in the dark 75

Chapter 8: The romance of the Seine 80

Chapter 9: Paris by bike 96

Chapter 10: Struck down 105

Chapter 11: Other people's lives 111

Chapter 12: Who let the dogs out? 116

Chapter 13: Breaking records 127

Chapter 14: The cost of freedom 134

Chapter 15: Boat-sitting in Belgium 141

Chapter 16: Finding answers in the silence 153

Chapter 17: Chamonix – closed for business 157

Chapter 18: If a fence can't hold water, it can't hold a goat .. 162

Chapter 19: Coming home 169

Chapter 20: Beware the reaper 179

Chapter 21: Off-grid house-sitting in the Spanish Pyrenees.. 186

Chapter 22: Sorry, I don't speak Spanish 194

Chapter 23: Christmas Day – home alone 201

Chapter 24: Carrion eaters 206

Chapter 25: Walking with Alfie 214

Chapter 26: Beware the boulangerie 220

Chapter 27: Musings from a settled life – but not for long 228

Chapter 28: Why do we travel? 242

Chapter 29: What next? 246

Acknowledgements 249

About the author 249

Excerpt from *How to be a House-Sitter* 251

Introduction

❖ ❖ ❖

It has been almost six years since my husband Michael and I sold our house, bought a boat and began our nomadic life cruising along the rivers and canals of France. Each of those years has brought new adjustments, a re-evaluation of how well this life was suiting us and whether there were things we needed to change. This book reflects the way our scope has broadened. We travel by bike now as well as cruising. With the loss of both our dogs during these intervening years we have also been able to experiment with house-sitting as a cost-effective way of moving round Europe and found it suits us well.

My first book, *Just Passing Through*, was a record of our first three years on the water. This book, *The Constant Traveller*, continues that tale, beginning as we travel back to France expecting a carefree summer season of cruising and instead find ourselves spending three months under lockdown on our boat in complete isolation, the only people living in what felt like a ghost port.

Travelling on a full-time basis is now our way of life and as we become ever more attuned to the seductive rhythms of a nomadic existence I have been struck by two things. The first is that this habit of continuous travelling has become an addiction, and I have neither the willpower nor the desire to resist when the wind whispers that something wonderful waits for me around the next corner. Whether it be cruising into the heart of Paris or boat-sitting on a barge in Belgium, cycling through sunflowers in rural France or house-sitting in the Spanish Pyrenees, travelling has opened a window into the heart of each country that we visit. It's like going back to school but the lessons are never boring, never dull. Geography, history, politics and science come to life in front of my eyes, vibrant and startling, helping me to understand this wonderful world a little better.

The more I travel, the more I value the journey for its own sake, and this is the second thing that I now understand more clearly. The journey is what matters; the destination becomes a lesser priority. When on a boat or a bike there is no choice but to be a slow traveller. I take my time, each day being precious, and the more closely I look for pleasure in the small things in life, the more I find. All any traveller needs to do is take those first steps and everything else will click into place, although there is no guarantee the path will take you quite where you thought you were going.

To travel is to experience life, to be challenged and inspired, to be changed. I can think of no better life than the one I am lucky enough to live and it will be a pleasure to share it with you. Turn the page and take those first steps with me – the journey is about to begin.

Mary-Jane Houlton

Part 1

The lost years

Mary-Jane Houlton

Chapter 1

Living through a pandemic on a boat

❖ ❖ ❖

It was 2am and Olivia Rose *lay quietly in her moorings. A weak sickle moon hung high in the sky, casting a faint glow over the marina, painting a muted, hazy impression of the boats until clouds scudded across her face and everything went black. Black water, black trees, a night of shadows. Two figures emerged from the side of a building, heads down, walking fast. They came to the locked gate that led down onto the pontoons where the boats were moored and as they stopped, taking time for a quick turn of the head left and right to make sure they were alone, the moon freed herself from the clouds and drew a sharp outline around them. Two men, young, black jeans, black hoodies, and one of them carried something long and thin in one hand, perhaps a crowbar.*

They paid no attention to the gate, inching themselves round the side, vaulting over the railings and tightrope-walking across the metal struts that bound the pontoons to the shore. It took only seconds. They were soft on their feet, each footfall considered and silent. Their pace slowed as they assessed the boats and as they came level with Olivia Rose, *they looked at each other in silent agreement. Crouching close to the side of the boat one man lifted the crowbar and jimmied our old wooden door off its hinges. Now they were inside. A few steps more took them to our bedroom and as they pushed the door open it creaked, loud in the silence.*

I woke with a jolt, eyes wide, heart pounding, stomach clenching. Disorientated and confused, instinct took over and my left hand closed about the rolling pin that I had placed by my bed the night before whilst my other hand flicked on the light switch. The room was empty. There were no shadowy figures by the bed.

'What are you doing?' Michael lifted his head blearily, saw the rolling pin in my hand, and sat up. 'What's wrong?'

'I don't know.' I waved the rolling pin towards the door. 'I thought I heard...' I trailed off.

Michael took the rolling pin from me and went to the door. A second later the light in the wheelhouse came on and I got out of bed and stood by him. The door was firmly on its hinges. We were alone.

'Bad dream?' he asked.

I nodded.

'Well, there's nothing to worry about. Come back to bed.'

'I'll be there in a minute. I might have a cup of tea first.'

There was a reason why I had gone to bed with a rolling pin by my side and some justification for the nightmare. *Olivia Rose* had indeed been broken into, a fortnight before we arrived. They had lifted our sliding door off its hinges to get in, stolen our good knives that we kept for cutting the mooring ropes if we got caught in a lock, broken a few things indiscriminately and let off a fire extinguisher which had made a mess but not done any real damage. The only thing of value on the boat had been our bikes, chained and padlocked down in the galley, but these had not been touched. Another boat had also been broken into, a much more expensive one with secure locks and heavy-duty doors. It would cost the owner several thousand euros to repair broken doors and smashed windows, whilst it cost us nothing. There is a perverse benefit to having a boat that is easily broken into.

No-one had any idea who had done it, or why, and the security cameras had naturally been pointing in the wrong direction at the time it happened. We put it down to lads out looking for a bit of trouble and hoped they wouldn't come back. Besides, we soon had far more important things to worry about.

It was 14th March 2020 and we had arrived back in France from the UK two days before, our journey a rushed affair due to concern over what effect the Coronavirus might have on future travel plans. Within a few short weeks it had grown from a far-off problem in China to a much more serious threat on our own doorstep. Whatever lay ahead, we knew we wanted to face it in France and on our boat. She was our home.

Two days later, France went into lockdown. The day began normally enough. There was a muted hum of traffic from the road, children were playing in a nearby playground and we could hear the intermittent beeping of a forklift truck in a nearby scrapyard. And then, at midday, which is when the lockdown officially began, silence fell. It wasn't a gradual lessening of noise but an abrupt, overwhelming emptiness. The cars all disappeared. The children never came back from their lunch break. The metal gates at the scrapyard stayed shut and the machines were still. No cyclists along the river banks, nobody strolling along the footpaths. Because we had arrived before the season had started, we were the only people living on their boat at the marina and from now on no-one would be allowed to visit. Our isolation was complete. We were swallowed up in the sound of the silence and nothing has ever felt so strange.

'Lockdown' is just a word and until that point in my life it wasn't part of my vocabulary at all. Now that one word governed our lives. Each country developed their own response to the pandemic and France clamped down hard on her people. Perhaps not surprisingly, given their love-hate relationship with paperwork and bureaucracy, form-filling was part of the package. No-one was allowed to leave their house without filling in a certificate of travel exemption, an *attestation de déplacement dérogatoire*, and 100,000 police officers were deployed to make sure everyone obeyed the rules. The form stated the five reasons we could be seen on the streets: essential work, purchasing food or medicines, doctor or hospital visits that couldn't be done remotely, supporting vulnerable family members/childcare and, lastly, physical activity and dog walking where people should keep one metre apart and walk no further than one kilometre or for one hour per day. Cycling to work or the shops was allowed if that was your only means of transport but cycling for pleasure was not permitted. We were supposed to fill in a new form each time we left the house, tick the box that gave the reason we were outside, note the time we left, and sign and date the form. Everyone was legally required to carry the form at all times and there was a fine of 135€ for non-compliance.

We ran into the police on our first visit to the *boulangerie*, walking with our dog Maddie to buy our bread for the day. The *capitaine* of the port had kindly supplied us with a bunch of photocopies of the form before he closed the office down and left for home, which is where he would carry on with the administrative side of running the marina for the foreseeable future. We had reluctantly taken two forms with us, one each as sharing wasn't allowed, but, given that it was barely a ten-minute walk from the boat, we hadn't bothered to fill in the date or time. The whole concept of needing paperwork on this level seemed ridiculous, completely alien.

The police car cruised slowly past, slowed down and then stopped.

'Why do I feel like I've done something wrong?' I muttered under my breath.

'We've got a dog to walk and essential food to get. Two good reasons to be here,' said Michael but I could tell he felt uneasy.

As we drew level the window came down and a uniformed arm appeared, hand outstretched. It seemed they wanted to look at our forms. I explained that we were just going to buy bread. He gave me the sort of look you get from policemen the world over and pointed at the empty space where the time and the date was meant to have been written.

'You must fill this in,' he said. He tapped a finger on it to make the point. 'Also, you cannot go out together. Only one person from each house at any one time.'

We looked at him in astonishment. This was the first we'd heard of this.

'Not even for a walk? Along the river? What harm can it do?'

'No.' He gave me a stern look. 'The only time you can be away from your home together is if one of you is ill and the other has to drive them to the hospital.' He handed the form back. 'Today, you can stay together, but no more after that.'

We bought our bread, not that there was much on the shelves, and walked back to the boat with glum faces, at a loss to understand how we could no longer do something so ordinary and yet suddenly so precious as to take a walk together in the open air. I saw the *gendarmerie* again the next day as I walked Maddie by myself along the river. They were patrolling the cycle track but they didn't stop me this time.

We came to detest that form, even more than having to wear a mask whenever we went into a shop or public place. It was a tangible sign of oppression and seemed way over the top. We weren't the only people struggling to come to terms with these new rules. One week after the forms were introduced almost 92,000 violations were reported. Steeper fines were imposed for repeat offences, even a prison sentence for extreme cases.

A few days later the authorities amended the rules and allowed members of the same household to take outside exercise together, presumably because somebody finally realised how illogical and stupid it was. Gathering in small groups was still banned however, so a family of four or more would have to walk in shifts, and the one-kilometre or one-hour rule stayed in place.

Food shopping became a stressful affair. Having seen pictures on the news of empty shelves in the supermarkets in the UK and with stories of wealthy Parisians fleeing the city to their second homes, where they were seen with two or three trolleys per person and food bills of over 600€, I felt anxious as to what I would find as I pulled into the car park. Donning my mask and checking for the umpteenth time that I had my form in my bag, I joined a queue of about thirty people waiting in an orderly line in the crisp March sunshine. A couple of bored-looking policeman stood by the entrance, letting people into the supermarket in batches.

Inside was a regime of handwashes and one-directional arrows, and where just a few days ago husbands, wives and families would have been wandering the aisles together, stopping to chat with friends while their children argued over how many sweets they could buy, it was now a solitary and silent affair. A larger than usual number of men perused the shelves with anxious expressions, a shopping list in one hand and their phones glued to their ears in the other, waiting for instructions from their wives about what to do if the preferred brand of pasta was no longer available.

Despite all the scaremongering in the press, I found everything I needed. There were some empty spaces on the shelves but all the important items were available and nobody seemed to be buying in unreasonable quantities or behaving badly. I loaded the van up, returned the trolley, rubbed yet more sanitiser into my hands and took off my mask. Driving the short distance back home along almost deserted streets I saw people driving towards me, alone in their cars, but still wearing a mask. Nothing made sense any more.

Chapter 2

Finding a new equilibrium

❖ ❖ ❖

One of our biggest challenges was accepting a new equilibrium, and finding positive ways to fill our time, for time was now the one thing we had in abundance. Friends and family back in the UK occupied themselves with DIY projects and working in their gardens but we lived on a boat, thirteen metres long and three and a half metres wide. Our options were limited.

'My pillow is wet.' I lay in bed and scanned the wood-panelled ceiling above me, trying to work out where the water was getting in.

'Mmm,' said Michael absently, preoccupied with reading the news on his phone and not really listening.

I waited patiently.

'There!' A tiny rivulet of water ran down a groove until gravity took a hand and it plopped silently onto my pillow. 'You need to fix that.'

'And how am I supposed to do that? Sorting out a leak isn't one of the tick boxes on the form and the DIY shops are shut.'

'You must have something on the boat that will do it. Just a temporary job until things open up again.'

He sighed in frustration but I knew he would cobble something together. Later that day I prowled around the decks, scowling at my empty plant pots. I had eighteen of them on board and I usually filled them with herbs, perhaps some tomatoes and lettuce, but mainly flowers. I was itching to get them planted, needing something to nurture, but the garden centres were shut and so even that simple pleasure was denied us.

There were the practical realities of living on a boat in this situation to deal with as well. We had no running water supply on board, which meant we couldn't shower, use the loo or clean the dishes. We had drained our water tanks down completely before we left the previous year, a normal practice to prevent burst pipes during winter when the boat would be uninhabited. The water supply to the pontoons was also turned off over the winter for the same reasons. Now that the marina was officially shut, any plans to turn the water back on had been delayed and so we were unable to fill our tanks back up again. This could have made life very difficult but we were given a key to allow us access to the *capitainerie* where there were showers, loos and a washing machine. We also had a 25-litre plastic water container that we usually kept in the van for camping. It came into its own now as we could fill it from the showers and then keep it in the galley as a handy source of water for cooking and washing up. The electricity remained connected, which was a huge relief as it meant we didn't have to rely on the generator for power. We had a working oven, lights and a plug-in radiator for warmth in the bedroom. The rest of the boat was kept warm with the woodburner. We were perfectly comfortable and, although initially the lack of water was irritating, we soon got used to the new system. However, the shower block was on the far side of the marina and I always felt slightly uneasy making the long walk over in the dark, torch in hand to keep the shadows at bay. The sheer emptiness of it all was strangely threatening, not helped by the niggling memory of our recent break-in.

We have always been good at keeping ourselves busy but we had to dig deep to keep our spirits up through this pandemic and there were days when we struggled. Michael taught himself to draw, producing pencil sketches of the birds that kept us company each day, herons and kingfishers, grebes and swans. I made the finishing touches to my first book *Just Passing Through* and published it. Reliving the memories of our first three years on the water gave me hope that we had not lost that life of freedom, that it would all come back to us eventually. There was no doubt that living in a small space added to the pressure at times, but we were surrounded by water and a rich abundance of wildlife which gave me great solace and joy and kept me going on the bad days.

One morning a cormorant popped up outside the cabin window as I was getting dressed. It fixed me with a beady eye and then dived again. A pair of herons regularly flapped by, slow and majestic, their daily routines unchanged and probably improved by the lack of humans. We named them George and Mildred until we realised there were actually four of them, but as we couldn't tell one from the other we decided they could all share names. The river teemed with fish, undulating shoals of tiny ones that rippled through the water as one entity, as well as two-foot-long monsters that cruised like submarines and slapped their tails against the hull of the boat in the dead of night. Frogs hidden in the reeds clicked and chirruped like an orchestra, beginning quietly with one solo performer but before long they would all join in, and I would marvel at how such tiny creatures could make so much noise.

And then there was the river itself, its moods changing almost as frequently as my own. Some days it was calm, flowing gently past. When the wind got up and blew against the current, waves of tiny white horses would race along the river as if desperate to escape. I would sit on the bank and wish I could go with them. The water changed colour all the time, cornflower or cobalt under a blue sky, shades of dull slate on grey days. On a clear and calm night I could sit up on deck and gaze at a full moon, so perfectly reflected in the black waters that it was hard to know which was the original and which the copy.

Michael went out for a walk with Maddie in the week leading up to Easter and came back ten minutes later with a miserable face. Like everybody else by then we were ignoring the one-kilometre rule and choosing the one-hour option, which also got stretched at times. Walking and being outside was essential for sanity and some rules were meant to be broken.

'What's up?' I asked. 'Why are you back so quickly?'

'They've shut the river footpaths. They've put barriers up and plastered notices all over the place.'

We eventually found out that the tightening of the restrictions was partly because of concerns about everybody coming out in large numbers from the towns over the Easter weekend and also because the sunny weather had already tempted families to drive out en masse for BBQs further along the river, mistakenly thinking that no-one would spot them. Our small world had just got even smaller and it was hard to bear. As Easter drew closer the police started patrolling around the marina at least twice a day to make sure no-one gathered in groups and we saw police motorbikes at lunchtime as well. The final straw was when a helicopter began a regular sweep in the skies around the marina and along the river banks. We were living in a police state and it didn't sit well.

As we moved into May and the weather began to warm up I took my yoga mat outside onto the pontoon but it was hard to concentrate. The herons were pairing off and George 1 was having a hard job keeping George 2 off his patch. As we got to know all our birds better so we also became more intimate with their personal habits. Herons produce huge droppings. We might not have fully realised how big until we saw an evacuation which landed on the pontoon by the boat. It looked as if someone had tipped over half a tin of grey/white paint and each time they flew over me while I tried to practise my yoga I offered a silent prayer that bottoms would stay firmly shut until they had passed me by and were far away. We also had two pairs of Egyptian geese, equally obsessed with territory, although to my human eyes there was more than enough room for all of them. If they ended up on the same bit of water then a confrontation was inevitable. They would rear up with chests puffed out, wings flapping and beaks pecking, making such a racket that I gave up on stretching out my hamstrings, sat up and watched the performance instead.

By the middle of May the lockdown came to an end but life didn't immediately go back to normal. Regaining all those freedoms we had taken for granted was a slow process. Most shops opened their doors once more and we were allowed to drive further afield, although with a limit of 100 kilometres outside our own *département*. The river paths were accessible and cycling was allowed. The best news was that we no longer had to fill in the much-loathed form. Restrictions still applied to the parts of our lives where people gathered in large numbers, with restaurants and the travel industry suffering particularly badly. Masks were still part of daily life.

With some light finally at the end of the tunnel, or at least that was what we hoped, people began to stand back and assess what effect the pandemic had had on their lives. So many different experiences, so much heartache and sadness for those who lost loved ones. Perhaps one day someone will write a book on how people coped, collating all those stories of how the human race survived such a cataclysmic event.

Whilst for many people it was a terrible time, for others it had acted as a catalyst for change, a realisation that they needed to reassess the way they lived and worked. There was the beginning of a shift in priorities. We understood this very well as we had already been through this process when we sold our house and bought *Olivia Rose.* We had already made that leap, leaving behind the responsibilities of running a home and a business to live a much simpler life. We had found a life of freedom but the pandemic had taken it away, clipping our wings just as we were learning to fly. Looking back now it doesn't seem possible that we had been confined for slightly less than three months. At the time it seemed interminable, and on a personal level I struggled to find anything positive about it. The best thing to do now was to put it behind us and move on.

Chapter 3

The lost years 2020–2021

❖ ❖ ❖

We finally left the marina at Basse-Ham in the middle of June, now down to a ship's company of three. Our collie dog Lucy had died back in the UK six months before, leaving Maddie to carry on the baton of ship's dog. We may have finally been released from our *confinement* but things were a long from way from being back to normal. The usual anticipation and excitement that we had come to expect at the thought of a summer on the water was muted. We had waited so long for this moment and yet something still didn't feel right.

The daily maintenance of the canal network in France is never-ending, a Herculean task at the best of times. During the lockdown no-one had been there to repair slippage on the banks, to check on the automatic systems that opened the lock gates, or to inspect the sluices that let the water in and out. There had been no dredging of the central channels and now many were blocked with weeds, some so bad that boats ground to a halt mid-canal, trapped by thick strands of weed wrapped around their propellers.

For three weeks we tried to find a way through but it was hopeless. Everywhere we turned there was a problem: a tunnel from the feeder reservoir on the Canal des Vosges had collapsed and now there was a shortage of water in both reservoir and canal. For a few days we made stop-start progress, with progress reports giving conflicting reports as to whether they could repair it. Eventually they decided to close the whole canal down until the end of August and so we turned back. Friends of ours tried the Canal de la Marne au Rhin but it was so choked with weeds that they got completely stuck and had to be pulled through to a safe place by a passing van driver, who drove slowly along the cycle trail with a rope attached to his tow bar. Another friend made some small progress by repeatedly diving beneath her boat and cutting a thick mat of weeds away from her propeller. It took her an hour to clear it each time.

Because so much of the world was still closed to travel the waterways were unnaturally empty and felt lonely places to be. We were used to keeping company with many different nationalities in a normal year, particularly with the Australians and Americans who have a strong relationship with France and her waterways. Some kept their own boats out here, others would take a hire boat for a fortnight, but due to the travel restrictions we saw none of them. Instead we cruised past marinas with rows of boats moored up and empty and wondered how the hire companies would survive this huge loss of business.

After three weeks of trying different routes and failing to get through we gave up. Nothing about this year felt right and whilst the threat of the pandemic had receded it had not gone away. If it were suddenly to mutate and become a problem again we would be vulnerable and so we turned around and headed back to the marina at Basse-Ham.

Life still goes on even in such strange times and in July we realised that if we wanted to stay in France for longer than three months in any six we would need to be properly resident and for that we needed a property. In September we bought a tiny, one-room wooden cabin close to the Pyrenees in the south west of France. It was just a shell, with no kitchen, no bedroom, no electricity, and the loo was a bucket in the shed but it came with five acres of land. We had purchased it with bad grace, no more than a means to an end, having never wanted to own a property again, but the pandemic returned with a vengeance over that winter and our humble shack became a safe haven. Quite unexpectedly we fell in love with it. Out of this unforeseen twist in our lives my second book was born, *A Simple Life*, a record of how we turned it into an off-grid home and began to integrate more fully into the country.

After a winter of successive lockdowns we tried yet again in early summer of 2021 to get back out on the water in *Olivia Rose*. This time it was just Michael and I as we had lost Maddie in the spring. After thirty years of having shared my life with dogs it felt very strange to be without one but we had decided that enough was enough. There are only so many times you can endure that last, inevitable trip to the vet and we were ready for the freedom that comes when you don't have the responsibility of a pet. It had been our intention to cruise into a different part of Europe, beginning with Belgium and the Netherlands, but it soon became obvious that the time was not yet right. There were too many restrictions in place and all the problems that we had come up against in the previous year were still there. We managed seven weeks cruising, but we were travelling in circles, going over old ground just for the sake of it, and there were times when it felt a bit flat. We needed new places, fresh challenges for our travelling to satisfy us, and that wasn't going to happen this year.

❖❖❖

As we packed our things away, preparing to leave *Olivia Rose* and return to our cabin for the winter, I looked back over the last two years and tried to make sense of them. On the one hand it was all too easy to think of them as lost years, a time where our world was rearranged by forces outside of my control, not just the pandemic but Brexit as well, and where I was unable to do what I loved most. The freedom to travel, to challenge myself through exploring new places and meeting new people, had become central to living a meaningful life. Our nomadic lifestyle was something I cherished and valued more deeply with each passing year and I missed it terribly during the stop-start, on-off chaos of the pandemic, almost as if it was my oxygen and I struggled to breathe without it.

However, as the months passed and I was able to look at things less emotionally, it became clear that time is never lost, it just carries you on a different path and things are rarely all bad. As a result of Brexit, which had initially seemed a catastrophic event in our lives, we had committed ourselves fully to living in France, and that had been a good decision. Because the cruising season was so short during 2020 it gave us time to find our cabin, Le Shack, and to wade through all the paperwork that came with gaining our French residency. We lost both our dogs during those two difficult years, a horrible experience, but the freedom that came with that lack of responsibility would open new doors.

If I looked hard enough every seemingly negative event had a positive side to it. And lastly, we still had *Olivia Rose*, the most important constant in our lives. We hadn't spent as much time on her as we wanted but she was still there, waiting for us, and we were more confident that 2022 would be a better year. I liked to visualise each year of our lives as a jigsaw puzzle, the individual tiles coming together over the successive months and the end result providing a portrait of the year. Our wonderful life hadn't disappeared, it had just been put on hold, and with the benefit of hindsight, I could see that those years hadn't been lost at all. It was simply that the pieces of the puzzle had changed, the theme rewritten by events outside of my control, and so the final result was different to what I had expected.

Chapter 4

House-sitting – a new way to travel

❖ ❖ ❖

'The rabbits need a feed morning and evening, one handful for each hutch. And I also hand-pick a large bucket of grass from the field along the drive and share it out each lunchtime. Their water will need to be topped up every couple of days. Sheep and goats get a section of hay from the trailer. The chickens get one big scoop of pellets in the morning and half a scoop of corn in the evening which you can scatter in the enclosure but the turkey has his in a bowl. You'll need to keep both of the sheep and the goat out or they'll steal all the food – tends to be a bit of a juggling act but you'll soon get the hang of it. I shut the gate at night, but half of the chickens sleep in the trees so they take their chances.'

'Are you getting all this?' asked Michael under his breath.

'Some of it. Hopefully the important bits.'

We were standing in the middle of a field receiving instructions from the Norwegian homeowner whose house we would be looking after for the next fortnight, a large farmhouse in the hills above Castelnaudary in the south of France. She and her husband needed to go back to the UK for a few weeks to visit family and that had opened up an opportunity for us to come and stay. We had been attracted to this particular house-sit as it had brought back memories of our own smallholding days in Wales but we hadn't fully realised quite how many animals we would be looking after.

'The geese get a quarter of a scoop.'

We had moved on and were now standing near the pond where the geese lived, two of them, a gander and his mate. I've never liked geese.

'Do we scatter that as well?' I asked.

'No, their bowl is over there, halfway along the pond. You can just see it in the grass.'

The gander stared at me malevolently and hissed in a 'This is my territory and don't even think about coming anywhere near me' tone of voice.

'They'll get used to you, but it might help if you take an empty bucket and he can attack that instead of you for the first few days.'

She was off again, striding back towards the house and barns, Michael and I scurrying along behind her.

'The cats are fed in the barn. There were just a couple of them to begin with but at last count there were seven. They're all feral. No idea where they come from. Their bowls need to stay up on the table, not on the floor or Layla will steal their food.'

Layla was the last of our charges, a Pyrenean guarding dog, who had the run of the property.

'Layla gets dog biscuits and any leftovers from our meals. She lives outside but I sometimes let her in for a few hours in the evening.'

'What about exercise?' I asked.

'She sorts herself out.'

To prove the point Layla, who had been half-dozing by the door, lifted her big head and suddenly shot off up the kilometre-long dirt track that led to the farmhouse, barking furiously.

'She does that all day long. She and the dog on the farm up the hill have an ongoing feud. Drives me mad but it keeps them both amused.'

'Isn't there a risk she might get out onto the road?'

'She won't leave the property. It's her responsibility. Right, I think that's about it. Let's go inside and get some supper on.'

The kitchen table was covered in carcasses, newly chopped, and bagged up.

'We had a clear-out of some of the scrawnier chickens and

the rabbits this morning. This lot are going in the freezer but I can keep one of each out for you if you like?'

She hardly waited for an answer but soon had us helping to prepare the evening meal, after which she and her husband packed for their journey to the ferry the next day. We watched them drive away on the following morning and looked at each other. We were now responsible for the well-being of the entire menagerie.

House-sitting was our new venture for the winter, a way for us to travel around France without having to spend any money on accommodation. Given that we lived on a tight budget, it was in reality the only way we could afford to travel at this time of year as our DIY camper van was strictly a summer-only experience. We didn't get paid for our services, but we had a base from which we could explore a region. The homeowner gained as it gave them the freedom to visit friends and family without having to pay for expensive kennels or catteries and their animals could stay in the familiar walls of their own homes. It was an exchange of services rather than finances and the whole system worked on trust. The homeowner trusted us not to run off with the silver and we trusted that their dog was indeed as sweet as they said it was and wouldn't bite the hand that fed it.

It was a question of debate as to who gained the most, and the balance could swing either way depending on how many animals were involved, but we set our own parameters of what we were comfortable taking on, avoiding certain potentially aggressive breeds of dog for example. Most house-sits involved dogs and/or cats, often a few chickens, and the majority were British people who had settled in France. It was rare to have as many animals as in this particular case, although we had seen some entries with six horses or thirteen dogs to look after, which seemed to be an abuse of the system. House-sitting should not be confused with a free holiday but neither should it be seen as an opportunity to exploit people.

Looking after both a home and the animals that live there was a responsibility. Animals needed to be exercised and fed, some dogs couldn't be left alone at all, and most owners preferred that their dogs were not left for more than a few hours. Long days out sightseeing or walking were rarely an option unless you had just cats to look after. It was a compromise, but one that we were happy to make, especially as travel wasn't our sole motivation. Living in someone else's house and taking on their lives for a few weeks, meeting local people and learning the customs of the region, gave us the chance to go beyond being a tourist. It also felt completely different to staying in a rented holiday cottage, or a bland room in a hotel or guest house. This was someone's home, filled with things that had sentimental value and memories, which made it a welcoming and comfortable place to spend time. Lastly, but by no means least, having lost both our own dogs in recent years, house-sitting gave us the chance to enjoy being with animals without long-term responsibility.

This was our third house-sit of the winter so far and we had learnt that it took a few days to settle in, to develop the mindset where someone else's home could almost instantly feel like home to us for the few short weeks we would be there. When we'd had our smallholding in Wales it had been the animals who contributed greatly to this sense of belonging and the same was true of house-sits.

'He's incredibly ugly and yet beautiful at the same time,' I said, watching avidly as the wattle on the turkey's head changed from red to blue. 'I think it's a shame he hasn't got a name. He deserves one.'

'Here we go,' muttered Michael.

'How about Terence? Terence the turkey. It's got a certain ring to it.'

Terence wasn't too impressed with having to live with the hens, but he had taken a liking to a scrawny black one with half her feathers missing. She was half the size of the other birds, so poorly feathered we couldn't even work out what breed she was, in such a state that she didn't look as if she was long for this world. She had taken a reciprocal shine to Terence and would hop into his big feed bowl and share his food. It made for a comical sight and always brought a smile to my face until one morning I found the little bird dead on the ground by the bowl. We knew from our own experience of keeping chickens that they can die on what almost seems a whim, but it always feels sad. Terence gave no sign of missing his little friend, but then birds and animals rarely do.

There were ten hutches, situated on the boundary under trees for shelter from the sun, each holding two large rabbits that were kept for breeding. They were fine-looking specimens but as the days passed I realised that I have a deep aversion to caged animals. It is a matter of degree. You could argue that hens and sheep are caged by being contained in an enclosure or a field, but at least they have a decent amount of space to move around in and lead a reasonably natural life. These rabbits could hop no more than two paces before coming up against the wall of the hutch. It didn't seem much like a good life to me.

The keeping of rabbits for food is common in rural France, part of a long-standing tradition of self-sufficiency. We had often seen cages stacked against the side of old farmhouses, a bit like an Ikea bookshelf or display cabinet, but storing rabbits instead of books. Often they had less room than the bunnies we were looking after.

I walked into the field one morning to find one of the sheep lying down, breathing hard and obviously in distress. Its tummy was noticeably distended. Chickens might be able to turn up their toes at the drop of a hat, but nothing beats a sheep for waking up and deciding that today is a good day to die. I ran my hands gently over its belly and sighed. Walking back into the kitchen I told Michael that we had a sick sheep.

'Oh great,' he said. 'First the chicken and now this. Do you know what's wrong with it?'

'It's probably eaten something it shouldn't. A load of acorns came down in the wind the other day and I think it might have been bingeing. Now it's blown up with gas and very uncomfortable. All we can do is keep it comfortable and watch it. I'll try it with a bit of yoghurt and see if that gets things moving. As long as it doesn't eat any more it should recover.'

There followed an anxious twenty-four hours, with me traipsing up to the field every few hours, looking for signs of improvement and seeing none. I would stare at it intently and it would stare vacantly back, giving nothing away. The owner had given me the contact number of a neighbour who also had sheep in the event of anything going wrong and she kindly came up and joined me in a session of sheep-watching, but agreed that there was nothing more to be done. I went to bed that night with the feeling that it would be resolved one way or the other by the morning.

The next day I walked up to the field, took a deep breath, and walked inside the lean-to where the chickens spent the night. The sheep lay on the far side, nestled in some hay, not moving, glassy eyes vacant as ever. I sighed. It looked as if it had lost the battle and died in the night. Now I would have to let the owner know that we had lost one of her sheep, not a conversation anyone wants to have.

Then it lifted its head.

'You little bugger,' I said joyfully as it got to its feet, and gave me a 'Woe is me but I'll survive' bleat. Two days later it was back to normal.

We both fell in love with the dog, Layla. She liked to come in for a few hours during the evening, stretching out on the rug by the sofa, occasionally getting up and pushing her great big head into our chests and demanding a head scratch, until she got too hot and wanted to be let out. She was no trouble and did indeed stay on the property – until the day when she didn't.

Michael had gone out for a walk while I was writing. Twenty minutes after he left my phone rang.

'I've got a problem. Layla is with me.'

I looked outside to where she had been lying not ten minutes ago.

'She just turned up. I looked behind me and there she was,' Michael continued. 'She's chasing cars, trying to bite their tyres.'

'Oh no. Can you get hold of her?'

'She won't let me anywhere near her and I haven't got a lead anyway. She'll keep following me, but any time a car goes past she goes for it. She's having a whale of a time, and I'm getting a load of abuse from the drivers.'

'Can't you come back over the fields?'

'Not until I get through this village. I just hope... oh no. Here comes a lorry.'

The phone went dead.

I sat and looked at it, my hand over my mouth, visualising all sorts of scenarios and none of them good. A few minutes later a text came through.

'We're ok. Back in ten minutes.'

Layla came bounding down the drive, giving me an ecstatic, and slobbery, greeting after her exciting morning. Michael followed, looking more frazzled than I have ever seen him.

'Next time I go out for a walk, she stays in the house. I am never going through that again.'

None of our other house-sits have had as much drama as this one did. We learnt that the more animals we took on, the greater the sense of responsibility, but this was balanced against enjoying their company. There is something to be said for looking after just one cat, but after a winter of almost constant back-to-back house-sitting we have come to the conclusion that variety keeps the experience fresh.

There was another, unexpected benefit from becoming winter house-sitters. I have always struggled with winter for all the usual reasons: the short days, the grey skies and rainy days when my world feels as if it is closing in on me and everything is on hold, waiting for the spring. This year winter felt completely different. It had been split up into segments, small chunks of time that began and had a finite end, each one offering something different to look forward to. We spent two weeks in a small flat next to the Mediterranean looking after a cat, this particular fortnight near Castelnaudary with the smallholding, and enjoyed several visits to the Dordogne, looking after dogs and puppies, cats and kittens, and a pair of chickens who felt the house was as much their domain as ours and would lay their eggs on the sofa if they managed to sneak in without us noticing.

Then there were the days when winter wasn't dull and drab at all, when a hoar frost would transform the garden of the house where we were staying into a wonderland, made all the more fascinating because it happened on unknown territory. Spiders' webs became white lacework, draped over bushes, strung between fence posts or clinging to the rusty remains of an old water pump by the well. The dried leaves of autumn gained a sugar coating of ice crystals around their edges and by the pond the ornamental grasses exploded like a white firework display. At times like this I could love winter for its own sake, a completely different beast to the warm, wet and gloomy days when it felt as if all the life had been sucked out of the landscape. Life became as simple as the chill of the freezing air on my cheeks and the miracle of a blade of grass coated in ice. Sometimes this is all we need.

That sinking feeling, that used to arrive when the clocks went back and winter stretched interminably before me, was gone. Each month there was the promise of something new, and interspersed between our house-sitting commitments we had Le Shack to come home to, spending a few weeks with the familiarity of our own things around us before setting off again.

By the end of the winter, after staying in five different houses and looking after a total of eighty-seven animals, I realised that I was becoming addicted to this nomadic life, not just in the summer on *Olivia Rose* but all year round. The promise of something new was intoxicating, and although there were times when we might feel a little isolated because we didn't know anyone or where the weather was persistently depressing, I could cope with winter far better than previously, knowing it was only for a couple of weeks and then there would be a new hill to climb, a new dog to walk, and a new house to call home.

Mary-Jane Houlton

Part 2

A new beginning

Mary-Jane Houlton

Chapter 5

The journey begins again

❖ ❖ ❖

I lay in bed, half-awake but drowsy, my eyes still closed, wriggling deep into the duvet and holding onto those last few moments of being neither fully awake nor deeply asleep, an in-between place. I heard the muted hum of the water pump as Michael filled the kettle for our morning mug of tea. He struck a match and I waited for the whoosh of the gas on the hob, followed by the song of the kettle as it began to heat up. Soon it would be whistling, or screaming if Michael was distracted and didn't get to it soon enough. Cupboard doors were opened and closed, cereal bowls and spoons clacking onto the tiled worktop. As he moved about the boat, she rocked gently. It was such a slight movement that you could easily miss it, but I was looking for it, waiting for it.

There is a softness to being on a boat, a sense of being held in a living, fluid cradle that moves and breathes with the wind and the water. Of course you could argue that a boat is not a living thing, that it is just a lump of metal, glass and wood with lots of moving parts, but we all know that's not true. Our boat, *Olivia Rose*, rocked serenely as I lay there, and I smiled to myself. After a winter living on land, shut away behind walls of concrete and stone, fixed and truly inanimate, I savoured this moment each morning, a quiet affirmation that we were back in the best part of our lives.

'Get up, lazy bones,' called Michael from the kitchen. 'Tea is brewing and it's a beautiful morning. Too good to stay in bed.'

My eyes snapped open and I pushed back the covers, swinging my legs over the side of the bed and pulling open the blinds. Sunshine flooded in, rippling over the wood-panelled walls and ceiling. I threw on some clothes and headed up and out. The galley was empty, no sign of Michael or my tea, but I could hear him pulling the chairs out on the top deck. We sat there in contented silence and soaked up the morning.

The last few days had been trying, as we had sorted out the inevitable teething problems that arise every year after the boat has been left for the winter. It was early April of 2022 and we had returned to the small port of Gannay on the Canal latéral à la Loire where we had left *Olivia Rose* for the past six months. We spent a week painting the hull and doing all our usual checks, getting her ready for the summer season. Everything seemed to be in working order but we ran into trouble within moments of setting off.

The first lock was no more than a couple of hundred metres away from our mooring. I stood at the bow in my usual position, ropes at the ready, but as we approached it I realised that something was wrong.

'What are you doing?' I called back to Michael. 'You're going to hit the gates.'

'I can't steer!' he shouted back. 'She's all over the place.'

By some miracle we got into the lock without hitting anything but the steering wheel was sluggish and unresponsive, forcing him to turn it again and again to get any change in direction.

'Why is it doing that?' I asked, wincing as we narrowly missed hitting the lock wall on the way out.

'I'm not sure. And it's not just the wheel that's playing up. The rudder angle indicator isn't working either.'

'Are the two related?'

'No. The indicator is an electrical problem.'

I tapped the glass display for the rudder a couple of times, which may sound an untechnical solution to a problem, but experience has taught us that giving something a tap or a wiggle can deliver miraculous results. Unfortunately, no miracle was forthcoming that day.

'What now?' I asked.

'Maybe the wheel is low on steering oil. You take the helm while I go and get some out of the back locker.'

'Me? How am I supposed to keep her straight?' I squeaked.

'By turning the wheel a lot more than you do normally and then back again quick- sharp. Don't worry about going straight, just keep us off the banks.'

And with that he disappeared over the back of the boat, down to the swim platform and the oil locker, leaving *Olivia Rose* and I lurching erratically from one side of the canal to the other.

'Got it.' He reappeared with a canister in hand. 'Now I need a spanner.'

He had to empty out the entire contents of one of the lockers inside the wheelhouse to find the right spanner but eventually the oil reservoir on the steering column was topped up.

'Any better?' he asked, wiping his hands on an oil cloth.

'Not much.'

'Air must have got into the system. We'll keep topping it up and hopefully it will settle down.'

A few kilometres later we both managed to convince ourselves that there was some small improvement, enough at least to get us to the mooring we had planned to reach that day.

'I wish I was an electrician.' Michael was lying on his back with his head inside the fuse box under the steering wheel. 'Or an engineer. Or somebody who knew what they were doing.'

I wished we had a boat where we could turn the key, the engine would purr into life, and everything would always work perfectly. They haven't invented that boat yet so for now we put up with what we've got. By the end of the day, my non-electrician husband had rewired the rudder indicator so that it worked again, and had researched the steering problem to the point where he knew how to fix it if it didn't sort itself out.

The next morning we started the engine, which had sounded as sweet as a nut the day before, and then it promptly died on us. Up came the floor in the wheelhouse and down went Michael into the engine bay. There was air in the fuel filters but once they were duly bled, the engine started running, stayed running and we set off once more. After these initial hiccups everything seemed to be running smoothly – until the next time. It is a blunt truth of boating life that there always is a next time: that wiring, switches, filters and all the other moving parts on a boat can decide they've had enough and throw the towel in at any point of any given day on any journey. The trick is not to worry about things that haven't happened yet, or to dwell on yesterday's frustrations. After six years of being on the water it is a lesson I am still learning.

It only takes a few days of motoring without any problems for the frustration to fade away and, as we sat on deck with our mugs of tea gently steaming in the fresh spring air, it was time to think about our cruising plans for the coming summer.

'So?' I asked.

Michael raised an eyebrow.

'What's the plan for this year then?'

He screwed up his face by way of an answer and sighed. I knew what that sigh meant. Two years of Covid had robbed us of the ability to plan too far ahead. Even in the days before the pandemic a life on the water was a fickle thing, with droughts and floods, canal closures and mechanical problems a part of everyday life.

'We know we're going north on the Canal du Nivernais,' he said. 'Why don't we leave it at that for the moment? One canal at a time. When we reach the end of it we'll decide whether to turn left or right.'

I nodded.

Our unwillingness to look too far ahead was not solely due to a lingering legacy from the uncertain days of the pandemic. When we first began cruising on *Olivia Rose* it felt as if we had magically been transported to a different world, a world where we could pretend we lived in our own bubble far away from the cares and concerns of normal life. This spring that bubble was conspicuous by its absence. Instead we found ourselves travelling against a backdrop of war on the fringes of Europe and political uncertainty in France. Suddenly the world felt a different place; borders were being redrawn, rules were being broken and the natural order of things was falling apart. The sense of insecurity and fear out in the real world was too strong to ignore.

On 24th February 2022, Russia invaded Ukraine. The peace that the rest of Europe had taken for granted for so long was shattered and we all watched in disbelief and horror as the story unfolded, reported in detail never seen before thanks to our modern information age. I have the rare privilege of being born into a generation who has not lived through a war in my own country, and there were days when it seemed wrong that I should have such a carefree life when others were suffering. Despite all the press coverage, there can still be a sense of distance for those who are not directly involved, not just physically but also emotionally. In a perverse way it seemed right that there were days when I felt guilty for living such a good life, aware of a sense of unease about what the future might hold, for at least it offered some proof that I hadn't become numb to the horrors of a war that still seemed distant even though I knew it was not.

On a more practical and purely personal level the rising cost of fuel due to the war might curtail how far we could travel this year. On all counts it seemed best to take it one month at a time and make our choices when we knew what the immediate future held.

Much closer to home, the latest development in French politics was also a worry as, almost out of nowhere, there was the threat of a new party in power. Earlier in the year, it had seemed that Emmanuel Macron would become the first president to win a second term in twenty years. He won the last election as an outsider, offering something completely different to the established regimes but now, as the incumbent, he had inevitably become part of the establishment. Despite this, he held the lead in the poll ratings in the first round of elections, buoyed up by his handling of both the pandemic and the way France had responded to the Ukraine war.

And then, over a few short weeks, it all fell apart and everybody was looking at Marine Le Pen and her far-right political party with new and wary eyes. She had worked hard to change her image and to focus on issues that were in the spotlight and important to the voters but, behind that facade, many of her policies were unchanged and could have a direct result on us personally. Key among these were continuing access to the health system for foreigners, which seemed highly likely to be withdrawn, and to residency, where the situation was not so clear-cut. At the moment we have a residency agreement that lasts for five years and should theoretically be renewed without difficulty. If Le Pen came into power, with the overriding belief that France is for the French and that foreign residents, if allowed to stay, are governed by a different set of rules, then the fragile stability that existed after Brexit would be put under strain once more.

Thankfully Macron won. The final round of voting on 24th April 2022 put him back in power for another five years with a better margin than expected. However if you dig beneath the headline figures, 42% of French voters were in favour of Le Pen and that is enough to leave a country deeply divided. The problems haven't gone away and a great deal will rest on Macron's policies and achievements over this next term. Given that the parliament is also divided he will struggle to get those policies approved. The French have always been worried about the threat of the far right getting into power, but with Macron unable to stand for the next election and with no obvious candidate to replace him, it may be that there is no-one there to fight them. We were aware that we could be facing another fraught situation in five years' time, but for now we were happy to breathe a sigh of relief and appreciate ever more intensely how lucky we were to live and be welcomed in this country.

Around me the sun was shining on the water and a soft wind rustled through the newly opened buds on the trees and in the hedgerows. It whispered not of worry and insecurity but of new beginnings, of growth and hope and dreams coming true, and if ever there was an hour, a morning or a day to live fully in the now, then this was it. It was time to begin our journey. The Canal du Nivernais was waiting for us.

Chapter 6

The Nivernais – finding paradise

❖ ❖ ❖

We had been along the Nivernais in the year before the pandemic struck, heading south. This time we were travelling in a northerly direction and it may sound simplistic but things do look different from the opposite direction. After many years travelling through France, both on and off the boat, one thing was becoming more noticeable regardless of which way we were facing, and that was the slow decline of the rural villages and small towns.

In Cercy-la-Tour the weekly market had just four stalls, a butcher, a greengrocer, and two cheesemakers and a trickle of customers that could never have generated enough income to make it worthwhile. In Clamécy we saw an entire residential street up for sale, despite the fact that the heart of the town still seemed busy. It confirmed our suspicion that a vital human element was quietly fading away in parts of France. Of course we were strangers, always passing through, and so perhaps we never saw the whole story, but there was no denying the empty windows in main streets as businesses like pharmacies, butchers and bakers, the mainstay of any community, quietly disappeared.

In contrast the natural world along the banks of the canal was thriving. Familiar feathered friends became part of our lives once more: swans regally patrolled their patch, glaring at *Olivia Rose* crossly for nudging them out of the way, woodpeckers and blue jays screeched in the trees and old man heron stood sentry on the shallow banks, as still as a statue until a fish made the mistake of getting too close and found itself expertly skewered on that needle-sharp beak. Coypus nibbled away at the greenery, outsize teeth reminding me of a Bugs Bunny cartoon from my childhood, and storks made their nests high in the branches above us.

White Charolais cattle grazed lazily in the long grass, knee-high in buttercups, and glossy, fine-boned brood mares nursed young foals. A profusion of dandelion seed heads, so many of them that it looked as if they had been sown as a crop rather than a random sprinkling of seed by the wind, blanketed entire fields, a dusting of icing sugar against the vivid green that only comes in the spring.

As spring eased itself gently towards summer the temperatures rose from the low to the mid-twenties, and it was time to bring out the shorts and the white legs. We spent our evenings moored up in small ports or, more frequently, alongside the bank by ourselves in the middle of nowhere, sitting out on deck until darkness softly fell. If there was such a thing as a paradise on earth, we had found our Eden.

We stayed for a week in Clamécy, partly because it was a charming little town and partly because we had business to attend to, an unavoidable and unwelcome intrusion on these idyllic days. Our newly acquired *carte de séjour*, a form of residential permit created in response to Brexit, allowed us to stay in France on a full-time basis for five years, after which we would need to renew it. With that residency came responsibilities and one of these entailed becoming part of the tax system. The French tax year runs from January to December and the tax return for 2021, our first full year of living in the country as residents, was due for submission.

In a country where its citizens have learnt to accept bureaucracy and the mountain of paperwork that follows in its footsteps with weary resignation, the complexity of the annual tax return is regarded as one step too far.

We had hoped to lighten our own burden by instructing an accountant to do this first tax return for us but we couldn't find one. Those that were recommended by other British people living in France were too busy to take on new clients. Looking online we found quotations ranging from £50 to £1000, neither of which were realistic or promoted confidence. Finally, with much reluctance, we decided to do it ourselves.

Calling it a tax return in the singular is misleading. There is one overall summary return, backed up by any number of supplementary returns depending on where your income comes from, what investments and bank accounts you hold, any other properties you own and so on. The supporting documents which I assume the author fondly, but wrongly, imagined might help to explain which boxes to tick and how to work out the maths are even more numerous and utterly incomprehensible even if you understand the language. We purchased an online guide written in English to navigate our way through. Given that I have a greater grasp of the French language than Michael this particular task fell to me, one of the few occasions when the royal 'we' was not in my favour.

The hours that I spent on this turned into days but finally I had done as much as I could. I still had questions to which only the French tax office could provide the answers and so we made an appointment at the local office in Clamécy. One good thing about the system here is that almost every town has a tax office and will see you even if you live elsewhere. They also had the reputation for being helpful and so we booked ourselves a mid-morning slot and waited to see how we got on.

'Are we ready?' asked Michael.

'As we'll ever be,' I replied. I checked my bag for the thick bundle of forms that I had already prepared, with question marks against the bits that still defeated both me and my new best friend 'Google Translate'. Then I double-checked that we had numerous forms of proof of identity: passports, driving licences, proof of residency, marriage and birth certificates, having learnt already never go to a formal meeting without them. The last piece of paper was a list of French vocabulary specifically relating to tax and financial matters which I almost knew by heart but it was there as a prompt if I went completely blank in the excitement of the moment. Satisfied that I had everything I might need, I took a deep breath and off we went.

The receptionist in the office took our name and told us to take a seat as the advisor was still with the previous appointment. This was obvious to us as we could hear her through the closed door.

'I think she's shouting at somebody,' I whispered to Michael.

The door opened and a small woman strode fiercely over to the receptionist, remonstrated with her about something – judging from the look on the receptionist's face she didn't appreciate it – and then disappeared back inside her office. Five minutes later the door opened and her previous visitor left, looking traumatised after their ordeal. Now it was our turn.

'*Madame, madame.*' She interrupted me as I was in mid-sentence, trying to explain our background and which bits of the form we needed help with. 'Do you actually live here? In France?'

I replied that we did, resisting the impulse to say that if we didn't we live here we wouldn't need to fill in the form and wouldn't be sitting in her office in the first place. She looked at me doubtfully and then gestured imperiously for me to hand over my forms.

It went downhill from there onwards. She ran a bony finger down the boxes that I had filled in already, muttering to herself as she did so, her French so fast that I had not the slightest idea what she said or if she was even talking to me. Then she got to the boxes with my question marks, jabbed a finger on them and glared at me.

'This is in the wrong place.' She turned to her screen. 'But I don't know where it should go.' She pulled up a copy of the advisory notes and scrolled down through the many, many pages that I had already spent hours poring over for enlightenment that never came. After much shrugging and frowning she reached some sort of conclusion.

'Here.' She pushed our paper version back through a slot at the bottom of the glass screen that separated us, and scrawled a couple of marks on two of the boxes. 'You move this one there, and the other one over here. Or at least I think so. Anything else?'

I looked at the outstanding questions on my notepad. It didn't seem worth the bother.

'No thank you. I think that will be quite enough.' I gathered my papers together and realised that one set was still on her side of the glass. I asked for them back.

'Mais non,' she said. 'These are my papers, not yours.'

'They definitely belong to me and I would like them back,' I said.

'No, I gave you back...'

'Madame, they are our papers.' I fixed her with the sort of look that only a woman who had wasted hours of her life trying to work out how to fill in these accursed forms might resort to. I knew these forms intimately and one set was definitely not back in my hands where they belonged. She opened her mouth to argue, thought better of it, and thrust the papers back across the table. The interview was over.

'That was a complete waste of time,' I said, fuming, as we walked back to the boat. 'And I don't agree with what she said either. She didn't really know what to do and I know enough by now to realise that she contradicted herself.'

The next day I finished off the forms as best as I could, stuffed them in an envelope and shoved them in the post. I dreaded to think what the response would be once our local tax office back at Le Shack received them, but for now I was past caring. Let them do their worst. As a final point on the subject and, in defence of the French people, we were unlucky with our advisor that day. If we had been assigned a more helpful person, which so many people are, it would have been a very different outcome.

Aside from the tax office experience, Clamécy was a pleasant place to spend a few days. You could walk around the centre in less than an hour, but to do so would be to miss out on the fine details, the hidden places in the backstreets. Each time I walked in to buy some bread or a slice of quiche for lunch I would pick a different alleyway for the return journey, marvelling at the medieval architecture, or stumbling across yet another café and wondering how such a small town could support so many eating establishments. Given that most of them only opened for one day a week during the time we were there, I guess they must have made all their money in high season.

Described as the gateway to Burgundy, Clamécy's claim to fame is that it was a vital point for the 'flottage' method of transporting timber from the Morvan forests to Paris in the sixteenth century. Seasoned beech and oak logs roughly one metre long were collected in the autumn and stacked in piles at twenty-two 'casting ports' along the upper reaches of the River Yonne. They were left to dry for the winter and then in the March of the following year the logs at all of the collecting stations were thrown into the river at the same time. It must have been an amazing sight as the artificially dammed water was released and the logs tumbled into the river, filling it from shore to shore, like so many giant matchsticks twisting and turning in the roiling waters. A cleverly designed water management system carried them to Clamécy where they ran up against a series of dams designed to halt their passage. At this point every single log was taken out of the water, identifiable to their owners by special marks cut in the wood.

Old black and white pictures at the Art and History Museum in the town show women and children working alongside the men, their long skirts trailing in the mud. It was heavy, hard and dangerous work as the wood was sorted and then eventually built into huge floating barges, 100 cubic metres of logs to each raft, each raft 36 metres long with the logs tied together by cords made from hazel. At this point they were steered down river by a single raftsman or a *flotteur*. Keeping him company would be a young child, an apprentice referred to as 'the little lad at the rear'. It was a challenging journey, particularly when navigating the dams where one false move or a misinterpretation of the current could have fatal consequences. Once the barges reached Châtel-Censoir the river widened enough to allow two barges to rope together side by side. The young apprentices were no longer needed and were put off here to walk back to Clamécy whilst the raftsmen would be on the river for another eleven days. Once they reached Paris the barge would be completely dismantled, sold to homes and businesses for firewood and the bargeman would then walk back to Clamécy, a journey which would take him four days. When he arrived another barge would be waiting for him and the whole process began again.

The first barge was floated on 22nd April 1547 and this practice was continued for more than three hundred years. At the beginning of the nineteenth century coal became the primary source of energy and signalled the final days of the floating barges. In 1881 the intricate systems of dams and reservoirs that managed the flow and depth of the river so that it could handle the logs were abandoned, the victim of an evolving industrialisation of the country. You can still find traces of this old system in and around Clamécy, and one of the original dams or *pertuis* was a short distance from where we were moored.[1]

On the day we left Clamécy, I took to the towpath on foot. This next stretch of the canal had six lifting bridges to negotiate, some of them close enough to walk between, others requiring that Michael put the bow into the bank so I could jump ashore just before the bridge and then he would repeat the process and pick me up again once he was through. These bridges often led only to a farm or provided access to the fields and were operated manually. A small metal box was fixed to a post by the bridge and all I had to do was tap on the button marked with an arrow pointing up to lift the bridge, wait for Michael to drive the boat

---

[1] Source: Musée d'Art et d'Histoire Romain Rolland à Clamécy

through, and then tap on the arrow pointing down to lower the bridge again.

All was going smoothly until one bridge got halfway back down after Michael had passed through and then stopped. The instructions stated that if this happened the operator should tap the red button to reset the mechanism. I gave it a gentle tap. Nothing happened. I tapped it again, with more conviction, and then gave it a good thump but still nothing happened. The bridge remained stubbornly at the halfway point.

'What's wrong?' yelled Michael.

'It's stuck. It won't move.'

'How did you manage that? It's just a simple push button.'

'Why do you always imagine it's my fault when something goes wrong? I didn't do anything, it just got stuck. I'll ring the lock-keeper and tell him what's happened.'

'How are you going to get back on the boat?' This was a good point. The pick-up pontoon was on the other side of the canal and it was a long walk to the next bridge.

'You'll just have to pick me up on this side. But pick your place carefully, there's not much depth.'

Mumbling under his breath, Michael edged *Olivia Rose* slowly towards me and then stopped.

'What have you stopped for?' I asked.

'It's too shallow. She's touched the bottom and if I come any further she'll ground herself completely.'

I have noticed on more than one occasion that when something goes amiss on the boat, the skipper will put it down to the boat being responsible rather than the person at the wheel, as if *Olivia* had decided of her own volition to stick her nose into shallow waters. I have also learnt that there is little to be gained from pointing this out.

'You'll have to jump across,' said Michael.

I ran a practised eye over the distance and knew I would do no such thing. Jumping from the boat onto a bank is much easier than doing it the other way round. I resigned myself to a long walk and left the skipper to cajole his boat back out of the shallows and into deeper waters.

At one point as I walked along the towpath that day I had a sense of déjà-vu, a flashback to when we had cruised past here in 2019. We had found the canal full of dead crows, dozens of them. We had presumed that the birds had been shot because they had reached such numbers that they had become a pest and were fouling the timbers in the nearby sawmill. The rookery was still there today, a busy airborne settlement, the leafy canopy above me trembling from the endless fluttering of wings and the normal tranquil silence of the canal filled with the harsh cawing of crows. The towpath ahead of me was spattered with bird droppings and just as I had the thought that I would be lucky to get through without being pooped upon, a streak of runny grey and white matter hit me, expertly timed so that it splattered all over my fleece. I grimaced, but could hardly blame them. Perhaps it was some measure of revenge against humans generally, even those without a shotgun in hand.

Chapter 7

Dancing in the dark

❖ ❖ ❖

On Wednesday 21st June, on the eve of the summer solstice, we arrived in Auxerre, the capital of the Yonne department, marking the end of our journey on the Nivernais and the beginning upon the River Yonne. This day also marked the fortieth anniversary of the Fête de la Musique. The idea of fixing a day each year to celebrate the human relationship with music was the brainchild of the Minister of Culture, Jack Lang, and his colleague Maurice Fleuret in 1982. They felt that a nation of music lovers needed somewhere they could be heard and nurtured and so the first 'day of music' was held in Paris that same year. Since then it has become a major event across the whole of France in towns big and small, and the concept has also been taken up worldwide. It always takes place on the actual day of the solstice, regardless of what day of the week it is, and the French people put on their best clothes and turn out in numbers.

'I've wandered into bedlam,' I said, resisting the impulse to put my hands over my ears.

We were standing at a junction in the winding backstreets of the old town, the timber-fronted buildings painted in pastel shades and the roof tiles gleaming a russet-red as the sun slipped behind glowering clouds. On one corner a brass band, the members wearing matching bright turquoise shirts, was valiantly pumping out the sort of music that only brass bands seem to play, but they were being drowned out by a group of drummers on the opposite corner. Further down one of the alleyways, a country and western ensemble, complete with Stetsons and checked shirts, were crooning old American classics with a French accent and from somewhere unseen a folk group were fiddling. It was surreal, almost dreamlike, with violins, trumpets, drums and guitars merging into a jumble of sounds, all fighting to be heard, and it could so easily have become a jarring, chaotic experience but it wasn't. It was full of joy and just a little mad, a fitting tribute to the wonder of music.

Every now and then we would find a musician in a quiet spot away from the crowds, where they could show their skills, or lack of them, to greater effect. We paused to listen to a man with a guitar and a beautiful voice sing sad songs, whilst next to him a couple of big-busted ladies with floral aprons and disapproving expressions were cooking up some sad-looking crêpes at a small table covered in a plastic tablecloth. Along every street and in every alleyway flowed a sea of people, dressed up for the occasion in brightly-coloured skirts and crisp white shirts. Their voices became part of the performance, with mothers pushing buggies and trying to keep track of their children as they darted off into the crowds, gangs of young girls giggling together, arm in arm, awkwardly self-aware, while older couples strolled comfortably hand in hand.

Night fell suddenly and before its due time, and looking up I could see that the glowering skies had turned black. A storm was coming. No-one took any notice. At the top of the town, in the main square, the local dance club performed a tango, men and women all dressed in black, very serious, very intense. The sound from a powerful music system filled the air, and a large crowd had gathered. The thunder began as a background rumble and grew until it drowned out the music but still they danced on. Raindrops pitter-pattered onto the awnings of the restaurants, lightly at first, and then heavier, and the crowd began to disappear beneath umbrellas or into doorways, but still they stayed to watch and the dancers danced on. It was only when the rain came down in sheets, filling the gutters and pouring down the streets, and the lightning split the skies with jagged forks, that everybody finally conceded defeat.

We had no umbrella and so we sheltered in a doorway in the hope that the worst of it might pass quickly but after a few minutes we resigned ourselves to getting wet and began the descent back down to the river where we were moored. This old town became more beautiful in the storm, the cobbled stones glistening and street lights throwing soft reflections. The sharp outlines of roofs and buildings blurred around the edges, a real-life watercolour that had been left out in the rain, and as that same gentle summer rain soaked through our clothes we became part of the picture, now so drenched that there was no point in hurrying. For most of my life I have seen the rain as something to escape from, understandably so as it has usually been bitterly cold with a biting wind behind it, but on that night it felt like a benign presence, something I could enjoy.

Back on *Olivia Rose* we changed into dry clothes and watched the lightning flickering and dying. It was business as usual at the restaurant opposite, with the last of the evening's diners sitting under the canopy, finishing their meals, oblivious of the weather. The rain faded away and we could hear a rock band playing inside a bar further along the quay.

As I lay in bed and waited for sleep to take me I wondered at what point in our history we began singing, dancing, and playing instruments. Who penned the first song, who invented the first instruments, and how did we go from those humble beginnings to concerts packed with thousands of people and reality TV shows with millions of viewers? How I would love to rewrite the syllabus for my history 'O' level. Henry VIII and his many wives would be consigned to the back of the shelf and instead I would compile a list of questions that needed answers, questions that looked at our history but that still had relevance today and would explain who we were. If the subject matter had interested me there might have been the slightest chance that I would have remembered some of it all these years later. I started to put my first history lesson together, but didn't get far. The band was still playing as I drifted off to sleep.

Chapter 8

The romance of the Seine

❖ ❖ ❖

'It's decision time,' said Michael.

We were moored up in Montereau, at the end of the River Yonne. Through the arches of the bridge just in front of us we caught glimpses of the commercial barges chugging past on the River Seine, bound for Paris, many of them doubled up, some two abreast. Their wake sent *Olivia Rose* rocking, and I could almost imagine that she had perked up, eager for a new challenge.

'I think our girl wants to go to Paris. And so do I.'

For the first time in the last three years we were heading into new territory and it was a good feeling, a heady cocktail of anticipation and uncertainty, a heightening of the senses at the thought of the unknown, tempered by a tightening of the gut as this was a big river, a busy river, and we would need to be alert.

A quaint translation from the French original of the chart book which would guide us through this region summed it up perfectly.

'Navigation in the middle of all this traffic must be done with precision. The skipper should keep a constant eye on surrounding boats. No question of playing the tourist, slowing down or zigzagging to take photos while at the wheel.'

I read this out to Michael.

'Are you trying to say something?' he asked.

'Definitely. You spend most of your time looking anywhere but ahead, which is fine on some rivers, but not on this one.'

We had cruised into a number of cities over the last few years, Lyon, Avignon, Toulouse and Carcassonne being some of the more memorable examples, and it had taught us that arriving by boat was very different to arriving by car. It had an element of romance and of mystery that couldn't be matched by arriving on four wheels, jostling for position in stop-start traffic, breathing in car fumes, and praying that the satnav actually knew where it was going. I think part of the magic comes from boats being an ancient form of transport, with all the associations of heritage and tradition, evoking images of intrepid explorers risking all in search of what lay over the horizon. In our case we weren't risking all, at least we hoped not, so it was a rather watered down version of those much earlier times, but it was good enough for me.

It was roughly 100 kilometres and nine locks from our mooring at Montereau to the centre of Paris and we had allowed ourselves four days for the journey.

Along the upper reaches of the Seine we passed stately mansions with immaculate lawns sweeping down to the water's edge. Sunloungers and pergolas hinted at lazy weekends and elegant soirées, city folk watching the sun set across the water with a glass in hand. Many of these homes had private moorings with a motor cruiser standing by.

We spent two nights moored at the port in Valvins, about eighty kilometres away from the centre of Paris. From here it was only a short bike ride to the Chateau de Fontainebleau. This was my first visit to this grand palace and I think I expected it to be rather like a National Trust property from the UK, but probably bigger. How our preconceptions love to play games with us, setting us up to expect one thing whilst reality delivers quite another.

From my experience, visiting a National Trust property is not just about the property itself, but also about the people who work there. The people at the front desk are usually welcoming and keen to explain what there is to see. Once inside, guides are stationed at various points along the route, often volunteers, who are passionate about the history of the rooms that they patrol. I am slightly ashamed to admit that I cannot match their passion, happy to pass through but not particularly gripped by the history behind this vase or that cabinet, and so I tend to avoid eye contact in the hope that they will recognise they are dealing with a philistine and share their knowledge with someone more worthy of it. Notwithstanding my ignorance, there is an uplifting sense that the people who work, or volunteer, in these historic properties care about what they do, and have a sense of commitment and pride.

We walked into the admission area at Fontainebleau and found ourselves faced with a wall of automated ticket dispensers. We expected something old and historic in keeping with the age of the building and found instead the ultra-modern. It was more like a bank than one of the largest palaces in France, second only to the Louvre for its magnificence. We frowned at this wall of steel, not sure what we were supposed to do. At the far end a uniformed woman sat behind a glass booth and pointedly ignored us. She had obviously been to the same school of 'Don't look them in the eye and they won't see me' as I had, and so Michael and I spent the next five minutes pressing buttons, swiping our credit card and bemoaning the state of a world where there is no personal service any more, until the machine reluctantly spewed out two tickets.

I waved the tickets in front of the woman in the glass box and she waved her hand vaguely in the direction of a nearby corridor and then turned away, ready to practise her studied lack of interest on the next group of tourists who had just come in the door and were looking as confused as we had been. She looked utterly dejected, as if there was no point to her life at all, and we found the same reaction in the stewards standing guard in each of the rooms, who glared at us sternly if we veered too close to a 'Ne touchez pas' sign. I wondered at the work ethos here and what went on behind the scenes to instil such an overwhelming apathy.

Our first impressions were not favourable but, once we had run the gauntlet of the admissions procedure, Fontainebleau itself proved to be mind-blowing, a spectacle on a grand scale. It has been the residence of thirty-four kings and two emperors and is the only chateau that has been lived in by every French monarch for almost eight centuries. The sense of history and of tradition, as well as the sheer size of it, was overwhelming, and it was obvious that it had been designed to make a statement, to impress and, when necessary, to intimidate. Any monarch who could spend this amount of money on one palace would surely have an army and a navy not to be messed with. This subliminal message of 'I've got more toys than you have' was reinforced by the sheer size and number of the paintings that adorned every available wall as well as the ceilings, the priceless ornaments, the ornate sculptures and the sumptuous décor inside the palace itself.

On and on it went, room after room. Apparently there are 1,500 rooms in the palace in total, of which about 250 are open to the public and some of those can only be seen on one of the official tours, which thankfully we were not on (that's the philistine with the short attention span speaking again). I tried to imagine the level of wealth that would be required to build such a place and then to fill it with this amount of furniture and art. I was seeing just a fraction of what it contained and, with each room that we were herded through, the word that sprang to my modern-day mind, a word that almost screamed at me, was 'excess'. It was simply too much to take on board. I live in a different age, in a world where words like decluttering and simplicity are part of my everyday vocabulary, words which have no place in these imposing state rooms. It didn't help that I have always found the kitchens and the stables in these types of places more interesting than the state rooms but, my leanings towards the servants' quarters notwithstanding, I couldn't help but feel that this level of excess was somehow too extreme.

All buildings require maintenance if they are not to deteriorate and, scrolling through the website of the chateau, it soon became clear that this palace still required a vast wealth to maintain and repair it, much of it coming from donations and fundraising. The website provided examples of recent projects: two million euros had been raised in nine months for the horseshoe staircase in 2018, with 900,000 euros in the process of being raised for the restoration of the Porte Dorée. In 2017 a twelve-year restoration of the Imperial Theatre had gained funding of ten million euros from the President of the United

Arab Emirates.[2] And so the list went on, painting a picture of a money-making machine that would ensure that this astonishing legacy, this massive mausoleum to a world long gone, would live on and flourish.

I know that history is important, that in some ways it has made each nation what it is today, and that it is right to preserve monuments from our past. And yet, part of me wonders how far we want to go down that road; just how much money do we want to pour down the throat of an entity that has little relevance to our modern world? What does it offer in return, apart from being a tourist attraction? I am fortunate enough to live in France, but I am a newcomer and haven't yet earned the right to question how certain things are done. I suspect in that sense I will always be a newcomer. Wealthy people and nations are free to donate their money wherever they want and rightly so, and yet I still can't help thinking of the good that even a small portion of those millions of euros being lavished upon staircases and doors could do for people in need.

Twenty kilometres away from the centre of Paris the mansions disappeared, replaced by blocks of flats and industrial units, the unremitting greyness of it all broken up by graffiti, garish slogans of protest sprayed over anything the artist with a spray can and a death wish could reach, on bridges, on walls,

---

[2] Source: www.chateaufontainbleau.fr

even on abandoned barges. Disused concrete quays and rusting mooring dolphins told their usual story of changing times, of the decline of commercial shipping, but whilst trade was ailing it was by no means dead. This was still a working river, and we passed quarries with barges moored alongside, sand and gravel being loaded into their holds, ready to be transported through the centre of Paris as they had been doing for so many years.

There are thirty-seven bridges straddling the Seine as it passes through Paris for a stretch of thirteen kilometres. The Pont Neuf is the oldest, built between 1578 and 1607, and the Passerelle Simone de Beauvoir is the newest, inaugurated in 2006.[3] As we passed beneath them I tried to imagine a similar scene in centuries past, a time when the only traffic on most of these bridges would have been a horse and cart. If we were to fast-forward another five hundred years, how much of the infrastructure of our own times would still be here?

A homeless man crouched on the ground under a bridge, his shelter a pile of blankets beside him. He looked frail, as if a strong wind could blow him away, and he paid us no heed as we passed by, staring with unseeing eyes at the ground a few feet in front of him. This trip might be new and exciting to me, but his world was very different to mine and I wondered what had happened in his life to bring him to this point.

---

[3] Source: https://en.parisinfo.com

We had reserved a mooring at the Bassin de l'Arsenal, a former mercantile port situated at the junction of the River Seine with the Canal Saint-Martin, and one of the few places that it was safe for small leisure craft such as ourselves to moor up. The only way in was to go through a lock, which led to a port with capacity for 200 boats, raised above the level of the river and so protected from the wash of the commercial barges and *les bateaux mouches*, the tourist boats offering trips along the Seine. The literal translation for *mouche* is a fly, conjuring up an image of a water fly, skimming gracefully over the river. In reality the water-flies are huge boats, all glass and plastic, with room for several hundred people crammed on board, gazing out of their windows as they fly past the big tourist spots. They travel far faster than the commercial barges and can turn in a second, swinging their sterns out and creating a huge wave behind them. They are a truly impressive sight when they do this, as long as you are not a little boat in the immediate vicinity. The truth of it is that the name *bateaux mouches* actually has nothing to do with flies, but instead originates from the place the boats were originally manufactured, the boatyards in the Mouche area of Lyon.

We had been warned that it was easy to miss the entrance to the marina and that it was also important to ring ahead to give the lock-keeper time to prepare the lock for you. There had once been a waiting platform just outside the lock but it was no longer available and waiting for long out on the busy river was not advised. Ten minutes before our expected arrival time I contacted the marina and arranged our entry. They confirmed that the lock would be ready for us and as no other boats were expected we could go straight in.

'I can't see the entrance at all,' I said, peering anxiously along the bank. 'The chart says it should be here but there's nothing.'

'Watch those two boats coming the other way,' said Michael. 'They're turning.'

As we watched the first boat slowed down, made a sharp turn and disappeared into what seemed a black hole in the concrete wall. I grabbed the binoculars.

'What can you see?'

'Not much. But it's gone all the way in and now the other boat is following it. Ah, now I see it and there's a green light. We can follow them in.'

We began the turn, lining ourselves up for the entry, and the light turned red.

'Why have they done that?' I punched redial on my phone and asked the lock-keeper why he hadn't let us in.

'*Madame*, only two boats can go in at any one time. Sometimes people don't ring ahead, and whoever arrives first goes in. You can go in next, but you will have to wait for a few more minutes as I have a tourist boat who has to come down and they have not arrived just yet. *Je suis desolé.*'

'Being sorry doesn't make it any better,' I muttered to myself as I turned the phone off. And so we had no choice but to wait on a windy river, being tossed about in the wake of passing barges, trying both to hold our position and keep out of the way.

'I don't like this,' said Michael. 'She's rolling about all over the place and it will disturb the muck at the bottom of the fuel tanks. If any of that gets in the system and blocks the fuel flow to the engine it will cut out and then we'll be in trouble.'

I had a flashback to when our engine died on us on the Rhône and knew exactly how that trouble would feel. All the mystery and romance of arriving in the capital city by boat vanished in a second, replaced by one of those 'Why do I put myself through this' moments which are a regular part of our boating lives. It seemed to take forever for the lock to fill up, deposit the boats up in the marina and then empty out again for us, but at last we saw a green light flash in the darkness of the tunnel and knew it was ready. As the lock gates clanged shut behind us we breathed a collective sigh of relief, *Olivia Rose* included. The waters gently lifted us up, the gates opened and as we entered the most iconic port in Paris, if not all of France, the magic flooded back and the anxiety disappeared in a heartbeat.

'There are some beautiful boats here,' I breathed, gazing in awe at gleaming wooden decks and perfect paintwork. Many of them were worth a great deal more than our boat, beloved but undoubtedly humble by comparison.

'We're a bit like a donkey surrounded by thoroughbred racehorses,' I said faintly to Michael.

'Nothing wrong with donkeys,' said Michael. 'Less likely to break a leg.' He slowed down. 'Here we are. Berth number 122. It's going to be fun getting into that space.'

It was going to be a tight fit, sandwiched between two much larger boats, and mooring in this situation without a bow thruster to guide us in always made things more difficult. We had one but it had broken several years ago and we hadn't been able to repair it yet. I grabbed one of the fenders and went to stand on the bow, ready to use it as a buffer if needed.

'If you're going to hit one of these boats, hit the one on the port side. It's not quite so immaculate.'

'In all our years so far I don't recall *Olivia Rose* hitting anything,' said Michael. 'It would be nice if the crew had a little faith. And said crew would also be more useful with a rope in her hand rather than casting aspersions on her skipper.'

It cost 58€ a night for a boat of our size to moor in the Arsenal which was a bargain compared to staying in a hotel within a couple of hundred yards of Notre Dame, but it was also a great deal more than we were used to paying. Many of our moorings were free, and those we did pay for ranged from 5€ to 25€.

'Wow, look at this.' We had moored up without any mishaps and were now in the *capitainerie* paying for our mooring.

Michael was looking at a copy of the tariffs. 'It would cost us about 8,600€ to stay here for a whole year. The biggest boat they can take is twenty-five metres long and that would cost over 15,000€.'

To put those figures in perspective we typically budget for 1,200€ for a yearly mooring, but Paris is a unique place and can command a much higher tariff.

Michael ran his finger down the page. 'It would cost 350€ if we were to stay here for a week. It's pretty good really. Think what a hotel would cost.'

'It might be good, but it's way out of our budget. Two nights is all we can afford. We'd better make the most of it.'

Immediately in front of our mooring was a high wall with steps leading up to the road above. We walked around the marina and over to the other side, which had been turned into landscaped gardens with benches, grassy areas and a path that led up to the Boulevard de la Bastille. This was a busy road but the pavements were wide and had been turned into a series of pétanque courts. Every single court was being used, by families, couples, groups of men; there was much banter and laughter but beneath it all there was no mistaking the concentration and focus behind each throw. The French don't play this game just for fun, they play to win.

A few feet away from the pétanque courts I spotted a row of grubby pop-up tents, a makeshift village. As we drew closer I saw a pair of bare feet poking out from underneath a door flap. The tents were pegged into ground so dusty and hard-baked from a hot summer that I wondered how the tent pegs found any purchase to hold them in place and couldn't begin to imagine how it would feel to spend my days and nights lying in such an inhospitable place. These were the homeless people of Paris, many of them refugees, hidden away under canvas and yet in plain sight. Around them, people played their games, strolled along the boulevard, drove and cycled past and ignored them so completely it was as if they didn't exist.

Later, after we had sat on deck and eaten our dinner, we set off for an evening stroll. Notre Dame was a few minutes away, hidden behind barricades after the fire of 2019 had destroyed a substantial part of the building. A series of photographs and information boards surrounded the site, with images of flames leaping into the sky, of fallen, blackened timbers and of men in biohazard suits sifting through the wreckage. They looked out of place, as if the characters from a sci-fi movie had wandered onto the wrong film set. Reading about the work that needed to be done and the astonishing level of detail and commitment it would require was both humbling and inspiring.

Leaving the ravaged cathedral behind us we turned to the banks of the Seine. After the rigours of the pandemic Paris was booming once more, the tourists flocking back like birds on a migratory path. The tables at the open-air restaurants were full, with people queuing for a place, and we heard accents from all around the world as we walked past, but by the far the dominant foreign language was American. The quays that lined the river had been claimed by students, by couples, by groups of friends, laying out a tablecloth on the hard concrete and sitting cross-legged with crisps and dips and bottles of wine. This is a commonly-seen French habit, and it never ceases to impress me how the laying out of a pretty tablecloth can transform a rough old wooden table or a stretch of hard ground into a place worthy of a fine picnic and a shared evening with friends.

As the darkness fell, and the lights came on, the river became a magical place. Paris is known as 'The City of Light' and at this time of night you can see why. There are over 296 illuminated sites in Paris, the most impressive of which is the Eiffel Tower with forty kilometres of illuminated garlands made up of 20,000 light bulbs strung around the monument. However this is not actually the explanation of the name, and the true source comes from the mid-seventeenth century when Louis XIV installed gas lighting throughout the city in a bid to reduce the crime rate. With lanterns on every street corner it was hoped that it would be harder for lawbreakers to hide in dark corners and evade the police. It was from this point that the city became known as La Ville-Lumière or 'The City of Light'.[4] In the following centuries, Paris gained a reputation for being at the forefront of innovation,

---

[4] Source: www.the culture trip.com

a centre of excellence for both art and science, and so the interpretation became more than just a physical description, reflecting the spirit of the people who lived there as well as the city itself.

We strolled slowly past the restaurants lining the river bank, shamelessly people-watching, trying to guess nationalities from the clothes they wore and the style with which they wore them, a favourite game of ours and one we never get any better at. Many of the restaurants had live music and we caught snatches of jazz or swing, of popular classics or soulful ballads as we meandered along, strings of fairy lights from the restaurants reflected in the dark water. I've noticed that the French love to dance, not just in Paris but all around the country, and how I love to watch them. One group had taken over the street in front of a restaurant where a band was playing lindy-hop and jive music and we sat on a wall with other spectators, smiling at the joy on the faces of the dancers as they turned and turned about. Some of them were almost professional, so elegant, so effortless, whilst others had been drawn in by the spectacle with no idea of what they were doing, bumping into each other, laughing and sharing the moment.

I am not a city girl, but I was surprised at the strength of the emotion that Paris evoked in me on that night, a special night that I shall not forget. She is truly a city of grace and of grandeur, a city to fall in love with, and to be proud of.

Chapter 9

Paris by bike

❖ ❖ ❖

'I've planned a route for us,' said Michael. 'What do you think?'

I leaned over his shoulder and peered at the screen on his phone but without my glasses it was a blur.

'Looks great.'

We were going to 'do' Paris by bike in one day. Parisians might snort in disgust at the thought of condensing all that this great city has to offer into one day but you could be here for a month and still not see it all and we had to work within the time limit that we had set ourselves. The threat of Covid had receded but not disappeared so we preferred not to use the underground and the bike lane network was extensive. During the pandemic Paris, like many cities, had created temporary cycling lanes which had since become permanent. There were currently over 1,000 kilometres of bike lanes, 300 kilometres of cycling tracks and 30,000 parking stands, with plans to extend this infrastructure so that the whole city could be cycled by 2026. Out of a city of ten million people, a million of them took to their bikes each day.[5] On the one hand this seemed like progress but it had created new tensions between cyclists and other road users, pedestrians in particular, who took their lives in their hands when crossing roads.

We had decided that we didn't have to go inside every single church, museum and art gallery on our route (more snorts of derision), and that this would be a whirlwind tour not just of the big tourist spots, but the backstreets as well. We wheeled our bikes along the length of the marina and up onto the Boulevard de la Bastille and then we stopped.

'They don't hang about, do they?' I said, as we watched bike after bike speed past us.

The cycle lanes were a blur of movement: bikes overtaking, bikes branching off to the left and right, bikes cutting across each other, bikes going much faster than the traffic, which was not difficult as it was almost at a standstill, and each rider was intent,

---

[5] Source: https://momentummag.com, 'Paris to become 100% cycling city', 9th August 2022, Ron Johnson

focused and ignored us completely. These were not tourists, these were the inhabitants of the city going to and from work, and if we were going to join them we would have to play by their rules.

'You ready?' Michael edged his bike closer, ready to join the flow when an opening appeared.

'I hope so,' I muttered as I pushed off and started pedalling hard, determined not to lose my place behind him. He was the one with the map, or perhaps I should more correctly say the app, that would take us where we wanted to go.

Standing on the pavement watching the sheer mass of the bikes had felt intimidating, but once we joined them and became part of the torrent of wheels flowing along the cycle lanes, it became an exhilarating experience. They were travelling fast, intent on getting from their homes to their place of work as quickly as possible, and there were few obvious tourists such as ourselves. It was impossible to dawdle, or to stop and check the route unless you pulled out of the cycle lane completely, and so we found ourselves matching their speed, travelling faster than we normally would, and the adrenalin pumping through our veins added to the thrill of it all.

Eventually we arrived at our first stop, the Basilica Sacré Coeur in Montmartre. Standing at around 200 metres above sea level this iconic monument is located at the second highest point of Paris, pipped to the post by the Eiffel Tower which is 300 metres tall. Building work began here in 1875 and was not completed until 1914, the extended length of time meaning that there were no less than seven architects working on the designs and construction. It has long been seen as a place of devotion and worship, and was a pagan site before being claimed by Christian churches. When the Romans invaded Paris they built temples here dedicated to the gods Mercury and Mars and it was only when the Roman Empire eventually adopted Christianity that the hill became a home for various churches. It houses one of the biggest mosaics in the world and also one of the largest bells. The 'Savoyarde' is three metres in diameter and weighs almost nineteen tonnes. It was made in Savoie, which is where it gets its name from, and arrived on site in 1895 carried by a team of twenty-eight horses. It would have been an awe-inspiring sight to see how they hung it. It rings on special occasions only and is so loud it can be heard ten kilometres away.

The basilica is perched atop Montmartre, which means 'mountain of martyrs' and was named in honour of St Denis, the patron saint of Paris. The story goes that he was beheaded on the hilltop by the Romans but, not one to take death seriously, he picked up his severed head and walked off with it, delivering a sermon on repentance at the same time. A miracle indeed. He is buried in the Basilica of Saint-Denis which is the point where allegedly his body stopped walking and finally dropped dead.[6]

---

[6] Source: dreamsinparis.com/facts-about-sacre-coeur

With over eleven million visitors a year it is hard to imagine that this huge church could retain any sense of calm and tranquillity, but we arrived early in the morning and it was empty enough for us to feel a certain peace. Apparently it is possible to spend a few hours there during the night and I imagine this would be a unique and powerful experience. When the doors shut at the end of the day and the tourists all disappear, the Night Adoration begins, a tradition of uninterrupted silent prayer that began in August 1885 and has continued through the 1944 Paris bombing and the more recent Covid pandemic. To join this adoration you pay a small fee and register between 8.30 and 9.45pm. Availability is limited and so it is best to apply 48 hours in advance. Visitors are hosted in a dormitory and can sleep until a nun wakes them up to pray for an hour or more so that a continuous relay of prayer is ensured. A French continental breakfast is served from 7.30am to 8.30am and costs 4€.[7]

I wonder who can register for this vigil, whether you have to be a Christian, and how the church ensures that those present will have the necessary respect. From what I can tell from their website, which is very well organised and presents a slightly surreal merger between an ancient ritual and modern technology, it is open to anyone willing to dedicate their time to it.

By the time we came back out into the sunshine the crowds

---

[7] Source: www.sacre-coeur-montmartre.com

were massing and it was time to leave. Cruising back down the hill I spotted an intriguing name for a café, The Hardware Société, and as we were ready for a break we took a table. It was like walking into an Australian enclave in the heart of Montmartre. The original Hardware café opened in Melbourne in 2009, this second café in Paris in 2014 and a third in Barcelona in 2020. We sat at our table outside on the pavement surrounded by Australian voices, tourists drawn to a taste of home with a dash of French style, and as we watched the mouth-watering and creative breakfasts pass us by, I wished I had known about this place before I ate such a huge energy-giving breakfast on the boat that morning.

From there we cycled to the Louvre, paused briefly to watch the long queue of people waiting to go in, and cycled on past. The Tuileries Garden, Place de la Concorde, the Champs Élysées and the Arc de Triomphe, were seen and conquered. Some places, like the Eiffel Tower and the Luxembourg Gardens, were pedestrian-only zones and so we got off our bikes and pushed them. In the backstreets, where it was less frantic, we cycled past old-fashioned shopfronts with their names scrolled in fancy gold lettering and, as we waited at a red light, I lifted my eyes skyward to admire the graceful lines of the buildings and their wrought-iron balconies, the vision of some long-ago architect who could never have foreseen how his creation would fit into the ultra-modern city that Paris has become.

The local cyclists had a typical French disdain for traffic lights, sensing when they were about to change a second before the lights turned green, weaving across busy car lanes as if they owned the roads, impervious to the hoots of horns and shouts of indignation from irate car drivers. Such manoeuvres had to be undertaken with conviction and as the morning progressed I could see that Michael had taken this on board, possibly with a little too much enthusiasm. As we cut across a junction with a nanosecond to spare before the lights turned against us, one of the car drivers leaned out of his window and gestured in fury.

'C'est Paris, quoi! Qu'est-ce que vous faites?'

I cycled on with a smile on my face. We were running the gauntlet, daredevils on two wheels, doing what you did when you cycled in Paris. I may have been sixty-one years of age, distressingly close to reaching sixty-two, but at times like this I tell myself that there is plenty of life yet in these not-so-old bones.

The next leg of our cycle journey was along the banks of the Seine, stopping to admire the floating islands and looking for somewhere suitable for a late lunch. We wanted a snack, not a three-course meal, and options were limited. A row of colourful deckchairs next to a van selling galettes seemed an appealing place to stop but we should have taken note that we were the only people there. A galette is a simple yet iconic French dish, a savoury pancake with a choice of fillings. It is such a simple dish that, until this point, I had assumed it was not possible to ruin it. I began to realise that things were not as they should be as I saw my leeks being dredged from the bottom of a pan where they might have been slowly festering for a couple of weeks. My mushrooms were slimy and no longer quite mushroom-shaped, but the whole concoction was on its paper plate and in my hand before I had time to say anything. Michael had added an egg to his selection and with stubborn determination managed to eat it all, on the principle that he had paid for it and wasn't going to waste it, but after a few mouthfuls I pushed mine aside. Within seconds a pigeon landed from its nearby vantage point and began to peck at my imposter of a galette. After a few mouthfuls it lifted its head, looked at me in silent agreement and flew off in disgust. The moral of this story is to be wary of food for tourists – or take your own picnic.

That afternoon we returned the bikes to the boat and set off to explore the Luxembourg Gardens and Jardins des Plantes on foot. We might cycle past buildings at speed but gardens are always deserving of a slower pace. After dinner we were out on the streets again, intending no more than a short walk but the city cast its spell on us and we lost track of time.

'Do you wish we were staying longer?' asked Michael.

I considered for a moment. 'Yes and no. There is so much still to see here and I hope we can come back another time and stay for longer. But today has been manic and a little bit crazy and that is how I would like to remember Paris. Maybe we'll come back another time, maybe we won't, but these two days here have been special. I shan't forget them.'

Michael took my hand in silent agreement and we turned down another side street and then another, just two more tourists getting lost in the backstreets of the City of Light on a soft summer's evening.

Chapter 10

Struck down

❖ ❖ ❖

'I don't feel so good.' I flopped down on the bench in the wheelhouse, feeling hot and out of sorts.

'Neither do I,' said Michael.

We looked at each other and didn't say anything, afraid that if the thought in both our minds was voiced it might become real and something we would have to deal with. We had left Paris two days ago and were now moored up beside a disused commercial quay just outside the small town of Cergy on the River L'Oise. The area had recently been prettied up, with some attractive flats and gardens close to the boat, and so we had thought it would be a reasonable place to stop for the night. The local kids started to appear in groups from 4pm. Our mooring spot was also their spot, their favourite place to congregate on a hot July night and throw themselves from the quay into the water. Backflips and somersaults, jeering and hooting, the thud, thud, thud as they hit the water reverberating against our hull. As one group left, another would arrive and it was 10pm before the quay was finally quiet.

We had gone to bed hours ago, unable to sleep with all the noise but feeling too weak to stay up. By now we had no doubt that we had Covid. We were both coughing and had a temperature.

'How can this come on so quickly?' I asked.

'Where did we get it from?' Michael turned over for the umpteenth time, the movement bringing on another coughing fit.

We must have caught it in Paris, but we couldn't say where. We had deliberately spent most of our time outside, Fontainebleau and Sacré Coeur being the only places we had gone inside buildings and mixed with people in enclosed spaces. In truth we could have picked it up anywhere and there was little to be gained from thinking about it now. We had been so careful over the past two years but it caught us in the end.

'What's that?' I pushed myself up onto my elbows and peered out the window above the bed. I could see a pair of legs, banging against the side of the quay. A second pair of legs joined the first. We had company, two guys who had come down to the river to sit and chat and they genuinely seemed to have no concept of personal space, no idea that there might have been people on the boat and that perhaps they could have chosen a different place to sit. We have come across this before and in other circumstances would have asked them politely to move as we couldn't sleep with them so close to the boat. Now we felt too ill to bother, and given that we were infectious it wouldn't have been the right thing to do anyway. A few minutes later a disco started up at a leisure complex hidden away in the trees on the other side of the river. I buried my head under my pillow and prayed pointlessly for oblivion.

This wasn't the first time we had endured a disturbed night. It is an inevitable part of a nomadic life, one of the few downsides, and we had learnt to live with it, able to deal with the frustration in the knowledge that we could always move on the next day. It can be wearing even when you are fit and healthy. When you're feeling rough it can all seem too much.

'I can't stay here another night,' I moaned to Michael the next morning. 'There has to be somewhere better than this.'

'It's a three-hour trip to the port at L'Isle Adam and only three locks.' Michael was looking at the chart. 'Think you're up to it?'

I nodded. Both of us were feeling better than expected given our disturbed night and we allowed the treacherous seeds of hope to suggest that this would be a one-day event and that life would soon be back to normal. Unfortunately our new-found energy drained away with each hour that passed and by the time we pulled into the very swish, but strangely almost empty, port at L'Isle Adam we could hardly lift a rope to throw it on a bollard. Thankfully there would be no noisy kids here, and we could easily self-isolate, speaking to the *capitain* to gain entry and arrange our stay by phone. We had little appetite for food, and no energy to cook it for the first few days, but as we began to feel better we knew we had a good stock of food in the cupboards to get us through the worst of it.

After two years of living in the shadow of Covid there was a sense of unreality in that we would finally have first-hand experience of it. I have had proper flu before and been utterly wiped out by it, but there was the understanding that it was just part of our lives, something to endure and that everything would go back to normal afterwards. No other illness in history has induced the media frenzy of this one, or the collective sharing of experiences and fears through social media, and so now the constant niggle lurking under the usual flu symptoms was whether this would run its course and be gone, or turn into something worse.

Memory is a fickle thing but I don't recall ever having known such weariness, such a bone-deep exhaustion. I had no energy to read or to do anything other than stare vacantly at the ceiling between coughing bouts or to fall deeply asleep until the next coughing fit woke me up. After several days of this I finally felt well enough to drag myself up to the top deck, hugely grateful for the fresh air on my sallow skin. The marina was part of a new leisure development, surrounded by expensive flats bought by Parisians for their weekend breaks and with three or four expensive restaurants spread out along the quayside. Hunched in my chair, struggling to breathe properly, I watched the young and beautiful people of Paris meeting friends for lunch, raising a glass of cold white wine that I could almost imagine sliding down my poor, poor throat and being served food that looked so good I could almost taste it, or would have if I could swallow properly.

The men wore tailored white shirts and shiny leather shoes. The women didn't so much walk as float, wearing pretty summer dresses of every hue and shade, like a flock of bright beautiful butterflies exuding youth, glamour and health, the last attribute being even more galling than the other two given my current condition.

We should have been amongst them, not quite such young butterflies perhaps, but we were supposed to be meeting friends here. They were driving close by on their way back to the UK from a holiday in Austria and it would have been their first visit to *Olivia Rose* and a high point of the summer for all of us, but of course we had cancelled it. At some point in my grumpy musings about the injustice of life at this particular point in time I fell asleep again. I have no idea how long I slept for, but I was snoring so loudly at one point that I woke myself up with a start. I had this mortifying image of me sitting there like some dribbling, snuffling old dear in front of the fashionable crowd dining at the end of the quay and scuttled in shame back down below to bed. Within seconds I was asleep again, hidden from sight and able to snore to my heart's content.

Just as we began to come out of it, each day slowly getting stronger, we ran into a heatwave. These have always been a regular feature of summer but each year they are getting noticeably worse. Temperatures of 41 degrees on a boat stuck in a marina with no natural shade are simply awful, a boat version of hell and completely debilitating, but we had to be grateful we weren't in Portugal where temperatures soared to 47 degrees. Forest fires were wreaking havoc in Spain and Portugal, and down in the south west of France hungry flames raged along the edge of the Dune du Pilat. Holidaymakers around Bordeaux were evacuated amongst scenes that were nothing short of apocalyptic. The climate was fighting back, ever more tangible signs that the planet was out of balance, and our woes seemed inconsequential by comparison.

Chapter 11

Other people's lives

❖ ❖ ❖

You see things from a boat, snapshots of other people's lives. At times it could feel as if they were actors performing scenes from a play and we were the invisible audience. Doing the washing up in the galley one evening we heard shouting outside. A group of teenage girls had been sitting quietly on the grass near the towpath, but now they were all on their feet. An older woman had turned up and said something to upset one of the girls.

'How can you say that?' The young girl was face to face with the older woman, perhaps her mother, but we could only guess. 'You don't understand, you never understand!'

The older woman said something in reply, quietly, but

whatever it was that she said only made matters worse. In seconds they were screaming at each other, neither listening to what the other was saying, and the other young girls all came to stand beside their friend, a pack of young animals protecting one of their own. As the fury of the two women erupted into pushing and shoving the teenagers acted swiftly, pulling them apart, using their own bodies as shields, and trying to calm both parties down.

Eventually two of them managed to persuade the older woman to leave, one walking either side of her down the towpath to make sure she did actually go, whilst the others comforted the young girl who was now sobbing uncontrollably, collapsed in a heap on the grass as if her legs couldn't support her. It was an emotionally charged scene and we would never know what had happened between these two people to provoke such animosity and hurt. It was sad to see a relationship so broken and yet I couldn't help but be moved and impressed by the mature and sympathetic way these young people had managed the situation and supported their friend.

On another occasion we were moored up by a picnic area on the outskirts of Amiens. It was a pleasant spot and we decided to stay for a few days. I was sitting on deck reading when I noticed a lady walking along the towpath, her grey hair cut in a short bob, dressed in bright pink trousers, a multi-coloured jumper and a thick cream cardigan. The whole ensemble was finished off with a woollen scarf, and it would not have been particularly noteworthy if not for the fact that it was 33 degrees on a hot August day and everyone else had the bare minimum of clothes on.

She put her bag down on a picnic table, walked up to the nearest tree and leant her head against it, her shoulders slumped, weariness written in every line of her body. She stayed there for a moment or two, her hands resting gently on the trunk, and then moved round the tree and rested her back against it, breathing deeply. From here she returned to the bench, sat down and pulled out a pair of sunglasses. With her eyes hidden there was no way to read her expression, no way to know what was happening in her life. The next time I looked up she was gone.

When you stay in one spot for any length of time, particularly if there is a focal point where people can sit down, you start to see the same people and to recognise their habits. People walking their dogs in the morning and evening, office workers unwrapping sandwiches at lunchtime, and two men, each with a dog, who spent their mornings in the park which I walked through to get to the *boulangerie* each day and their afternoons under the shade of the trees near to the boat. One man was older, one younger, and I fancied there was a family resemblance, although this could have just been an overactive imagination.

Their dogs were a mirror image of their owners, one older and one younger. In the afternoon the older man and his dog would stretch out on the grass and fall asleep after drinking a few beers, empty bottles scattered in the grass beside them, whilst the younger pair watched over them. They were dressed shabbily and I suspected they might have been homeless, although they asked for no money and the dogs looked healthy.

I have often seen French people give money to a homeless person sitting on the pavement, sometimes even stopping to shake their hand and spending time talking to them. I have seen women come out of their homes with a cup of coffee in hand and give it to the tramp sitting huddled on the doorstep at the end of their street. They seem to have a tolerant, inclusive attitude towards people who are less fortunate for whatever the reason. On the other hand, people still walk by as if they don't exist, particularly in the larger cities.

There is a charity called 'The Collective of the Dead' which keeps a count of the number of homeless people dying on the streets.[8] Their records put the number who died in 2021 at over 500 people, ranging from 80 years old to young children, although they think the real number is higher, possibly several thousand. The charity has around 200 volunteers but also works with local associations. If they can locate the family of the deceased, they will get in touch, offer support and even attend the funeral if there is no-one else to go.

---

[8] Source: www.mortsdelarue.org

A few days later and we were moving on. As the town faded away into the distance I knew that today would be a day like every other day for those two men and their dogs. Neither of them had seemed particularly unhappy or depressed with their lot, but what different lives we all lead.

Chapter 12

Who let the dogs out?

❖ ❖ ❖

There comes a point each year when we go back to pick up the van, safely parked for a small fee at a boatyard not far from where we began our cruising season. This tends to be towards the end of the cruising season, but the precise time and location is decided by our proximity to a good train connection. In the past, Michael has gone back while I have stayed on board with the dogs, but now our dogs were no longer with us it opened up new possibilities.

'All the train routes from here go through Paris,' said Michael. 'We'd have to change when we got there, spend an hour getting across the city by train and then pick up another train on the other side.'

'I don't fancy going through Paris,' I said. 'I assume we can't get a second dose of Covid that quickly but I'd rather not take the chance.' It had been three weeks since we had caught the virus and we were only now beginning to feel like our normal selves.

'I don't like it either but what other options have we got?'

'We could cycle.'

'The van is 200 kilometres away.'

'We can spread it over three or four days.'

'And what about accommodation?'

'I'm sure we can find a couple of Airbnb places close to the route. If we pick one which is self-contained with a kitchen we can cook for ourselves which will help keep the cost down.'

'Or we could camp. That would really keep the cost down.'

I spotted the enthusiastic gleam in his eye and prepared myself for battle.

'And why would we want to do that?'

'It's cheaper.'

'We don't have a tent. Or sleeping bags.'

'Well, there would be an upfront cost then, but we could use them in future...'

'I get very uncomfortable sleeping on the ground. And supposing it rains. We'd end up spending the evening stuck in a tiny tent in wet clothes. I can't think of anything worse.'

'It won't rain. It's July.'

'It might. A summer storm. Thunder and lightning.' I shuddered.

'I think it's a good idea.'

'I think it's a terrible idea.'

Our marriage is peppered with discussions like this. We don't argue, we discuss. We go round in circles for a while and an agreement is eventually reached, sometimes in my favour, sometimes in Michael's.

In the end we agreed to do the trip over three days, covering sixty-five to seventy kilometres each day and staying in B&Bs each night. Having just come out of one heatwave, another was on the way, giving us a short window where the temperature would be in the high twenties before reaching the high thirties again.

On 26th July we left *Olivia Rose* moored up on the River Aisne, tucked away behind some bushes in a quiet rural mooring, and set off on the first leg of our journey. This part of France is largely arable, and we were cycling through country lanes at harvest time. We met more tractors than we did cars, rumbling along with their trailers full of grain, and at times the combine harvesters were our only other companions, methodically munching their way back and forth, back and forth, leaving behind them fields of golden stubble dotted with bales waiting to be stacked.

It was a peaceful scene but we soon found out that it had not always been so. As we paused for a drink of water Michael saw a noticeboard under a stunted, rather ugly apple tree on the other side of the road. Looking more closely we realised that it was a very modest war memorial and from the faded black and white photograph we could just make out rows of simple wooden crosses. The brief inscription stated that in 1918 the ground we were now standing on had been a temporary graveyard for American soldiers.

I tried to place myself back in the past, hearing the sharp, metallic crack of guns and the cries of the young men as they fought and died, but it was hard to reconcile this quiet and pleasant spot with the bleak photo in front of us. The same apple tree was part of the scene, instantly recognisable because of its shape and looking as stunted then as it did now, almost as if it had been frozen in time, but otherwise nature had moved on, the loss of human life of no more account than the death of an insect or a bird. Countless seasons had come and gone, the grass had grown over the burial site and, if not for that sad and faded photograph, nobody would ever know what had happened here.

We covered sixty-nine kilometres on that first day, our destination a small town called Nogent-l'Artaud on the River Marne, reaching our B&B around mid-afternoon. We were invited into the owners' house for a cup of tea, given a tour of the garden, introduced to the donkey and the turkey and then shown where we would be sleeping. A small barn, more of an outhouse really, had been converted into a studio room with kitchenette, a bed, a bathroom and a small patio area. We had brought a bag of pasta, some sauce, and a bottle of wine with us, not the most exciting dinner but after a day out in the fresh air even the most humble of meals can taste fine. By nine thirty we were in bed and sound asleep.

We set off the next day straight into a steep hill. The countryside on this trip was by no means mountainous, but it had its fair share of hills, which are always a joy on the way down and not quite so wonderful on the way back up. At times the denuded arable land, dry and brittle after such a dry, hot summer, would be broken up by belts of forested land. The day was warming up quickly and the green canopy, soft and cool, provided a welcome relief.

It's hard to avoid dogs when cycling through rural France. Some are tied up, and whilst they sound horribly ferocious, at least they can't reach us. But not all dogs are restrained; some are left free to attack the postman and any passing cyclist.

What have you stopped for?' Michael asked as I waited for him about a hundred yards before a farm.

'Shh,' I whispered. 'I think I spotted a dog up there, asleep by the farm entrance. If we go quietly we might get past before it realises we're there.'

There was a low growl from the high bank behind me. The dog was no longer asleep by the road and it wasn't alone. There were three of them, all mixed breeds, one with a bit of collie in it, another a bit of husky and the third with too much Alsatian in it for my liking.

'Time to go,' said Michael.

They shadowed us from the bank as we pedalled fast along the road, at this point concentrating on protecting their property, barking and growling, hackles up, but content to keep their distance. As we neared the entrance to the farm I thought we'd made it but then the leader of the pack, the cross-bred Alsatian, shot out of the open gates and into the road and started to chase me in earnest. I went to change my electric bike up into turbo mode but pressed the arrow the wrong way – I do that sort of thing when I get panicky – taking it down to the lowest setting which brought a set of gnashing teeth disturbingly close to my ankles. A second later, I got the bike into turbo and off I shot, pedalling for all I was worth. I thought the dog would give up after a few yards (they usually do), but it stuck with me for what seemed ages before deciding that it had made its point. It turned round and headed back down the hill towards Michael. Much to my surprise and relief the dog disappeared inside the gates, ignoring him completely. We didn't stop until we got to the top of the hill, both of us breathing hard.

'Nice of you to wait for me,' Michael panted.

'Every woman for herself, darling. Besides, it ignored you.'

'But supposing it hadn't?'

'Then either you would have seen it off or I would have come down and rescued you.'

Our B&B that night was situated in another town called Nogent, the similarity in names pure coincidence, this one being called Nogent-sur-Seine. It was a room in a terraced town house but we had use of the kitchen, which meant we could whip up another culinary feast. In fact, by the time arrived we couldn't be bothered to cook and got a takeaway pizza instead. The house belonged to a nurse, who had hoped to be there to welcome us, but then left a message to say that she had to work an extra shift and wouldn't be back until 9pm. She told us that the front door would be unlocked and to make ourselves at home. We could leave our bikes in the patio area at the back, although the only way to access it was to wheel them through the living room.

Trust is a wonderful thing. She didn't know anything about us and yet she trusted us not to abuse her hospitality and her home. And not just us. As we collapsed in a hot and sweaty heap out in the garden, a cup of restorative tea in hand, a young man came in through the front door. He was an engineer at the nearby nuclear power station and stayed here during the week. There were only two rooms upstairs, and we couldn't work out where the owner slept. Later we found out that she had converted a room in an adjoining building, a very small one, by the patio area. From the photos on the wall we could see she had grown-up children and that, for whatever reason, she was now single. Perhaps she let out her rooms to make ends meet, perhaps because she just enjoyed the company. There are questions that a stranger cannot ask.

We woke up on the third, and final, morning of our journey, looked at each other and, with the unspoken intimacy that comes after years of blissful marriage, both knew we weren't particularly looking forward to what lay ahead. This was the longest day and the one with the most hills. After two days of hard cycling, our leg muscles felt tight, as if another seventy kilometres might snap them, and our buttocks now permanently shaped like our saddles, not a shape they were ever meant to be.

It turned out to be a long, hot day's riding as the heatwave arrived earlier than expected. By midday it was nearly 30 degrees in the shade. The arable landscape had taken over completely, and without the cool forest or sleepy villages to break up the journey the hours passed by ever more slowly. The scenery almost became monotone, an endless blanket of stubble fields shorn of their crops, the tawny-coloured stalks and dry earth rolling away from us like dunes in a desert and as the heat continued to grow I felt like some tiny insect scuttling along a track, longing for a rock to crawl under. We saw fewer and fewer cars, the only sign of human company a far-off combine harvester or a tractor ploughing up the parched fields, sending billowing clouds of dust across the road. It felt as if we were truly in the middle of nowhere and it wasn't the most hospitable of places.

We huddled together in the shade of a single tree and gulped down mouthfuls of water, mindful that we had to ration it to see us through the day. I got back on my bike, wincing as my buttocks settled back into the saddle, and in a bid to think about something other than the next hill, pondered a while on the concept of being in the middle of nowhere. I've always thought I liked the idea, associating it with peace, with a pleasing landscape, with feeling at ease and being in harmony with my surroundings but as the barren landscape enfolded me, it struck me that there was a flip side to being nowhere, one that can make a single human feel vulnerable and insignificant.

In our crowded world, can we ever truly be in the middle of nowhere? I guess the answer depends on how you define it. If 'nowhere' is a place where humans have not made their mark, then the opportunity to find it must be decreasing as each year passes. As I looked about me that day, a tiny speck of humanity in a food bowl being managed on an industrial scale, it was obvious that mankind can create their own version of nowhere.

At last, weary but exultant, we reached our final destination, the boatyard at Migennes where we had left the van as we passed through on the boat one month and three days ago. Doing roughly that same distance on our bikes had taken us fifteen hours of cycling over three days, whilst the return trip in the van was just three and a half hours. It becomes clearer to us with each passing year that our mode of transport greatly affects our experience as travellers. It will determine what we see, the people we meet, how our bodies feel at the end of each day, and the sense of satisfaction that we feel as drift into sleep. Whilst cruising on *Olivia Rose* we have found that the experience is richer if the journey itself is at least as important, if not more so, than the destination. Cycling across the country over the last few days engendered those same feelings and we resolved to try to use our bikes more and the van less in the future.

'Fancy another ride tomorrow?' asked Michael, as I eased myself gently into bed that night.

'Nothing on earth would make me get on the bike

tomorrow,' I said as I sighed and stretched out. 'My thigh muscles would mutiny. But give me a few days' rest and time to build up buttocks as tough as leather and thighs of steel, then yes, definitely.' And with that happy thought in my mind, I fell sound asleep.

Chapter 13

Breaking records

❖ ❖ ❖

'There's trouble down on the Canal du Midi,' I told Michael. 'According to this news article farmers around Castelnaudary have vandalised some of the locks.'

'Why would they do that?'

'Don't know but the damage is significant and they've had to shut a fifteen-kilometre section of the canal because of it. The farmers have lifted the lock gates right off their hinges and the authorities are going to have to get a crane in to repair it.'[9]

As I read on it became obvious that this was a conflict over

---

[9] Source: RTL, rtl.fr/actu/debats, 9th August 2022

water resources. The farmers pump water out of the canals and rivers to irrigate their crops. The tourist industry wants to keep a minimum level of water in those same waterways so that boats can pass safely through without running aground. In times of drought there is an obvious conflict of interests. Stringent drought restrictions had been placed upon the farmers, limiting the amount of water they could take from the rivers and canals. However equivalent restrictions had not been placed upon the use of the canal for pleasure boating. Each time a lock is used it is the equivalent to half a hectare of crops being irrigated. It was peak summer season and the Canal du Midi would have been crammed full of holiday boats, with locks emptying and filling all day long. The farmers said they understood that tourism was needed for the economy and should be supported, but cutting off water to farmers and letting boats pass through without any constraint in one of the worst droughts the country has ever seen was neither fair nor sensible.

Some of the farmers felt so strongly about it that they had resorted to vandalism, scrawling the words 'Freedom to irrigate' and 'No to the waste of water' at the locks they had damaged. I could understand their frustration, their desperate need to have water for crops and for their livestock, although I wasn't sure about their methods of getting the point over. When resources are scarce, decisions as to who has priority and how to manage the distribution in a fair way so that everyone can accept it must be very hard. This difficult situation was an early warning, an example of future unrest as the consequences of the climate crisis become more stark each year.

The signs that we were going to have a summer of extreme weather had been there right from the beginning of our cruising season and not just in France but across the whole of Europe. In May we had the first heatwave of the year, unseasonably early, putting an ever-growing number of French regions on drought alert. At that point it had rained 35% less than the previous year and some areas were experiencing temperatures of 8 to 10 degrees C higher than the norm.[10]

By mid-June we were in the middle of another heatwave, with temperatures of 40 degrees and violent storms, often very localised, bringing with them hail, flash floods and strong winds. As the water levels dropped lower and lower, the canals started closing down in part or in full, or operating on restricted times, which was usually a precursor to closing down. The canals of the Ardennes, the Centre, the Vosges, the Briare, the Marne au Rhin, the Champagne et Bourgogne, the latéral à la Loire and Burgundy fell one after the other. Each year sees its share of problems due to water shortages, but this was something new. Some boats ended up doing hundreds of extra kilometres to reach their winter

---

[10] Source: *Le Parisien*, 'Ten French départements on alert for drought', 9th May 2022

moorings, finding one route barred and turning around to find another one had closed up behind them. The situation was further worsened by the perennial weed problem which had hit a new high in its bid to gridlock the whole system. The Canal de St Quentin was one of the few routes north that remained open but a lock-keeper was having to accompany individual boats along the canal as thick mats of weed were preventing the lock gates from opening and shutting. Propellers were being jammed and water intake filters were getting clogged, causing all manner of problems. That had been our intended route north, but now we were forced to think again.

'Whatever happened to stress-free cruising,' I grumbled to myself, a map of the waterways in France spread out on the table in front of me as I tried to work out a different route north. 'I think we're going to have no choice but to take the Canal du Nord.'

'Marvellous,' said Michael gloomily.

Our waterways guide for the Canal du Nord had an interesting paragraph about the navigation conditions and moorings for pleasure boats.

'*This canal is heavily used by barges going between the dense northern canals and the Parisian basin. The sloped concrete banks reflect the waves of a passing boat for quite a long time. As you go past a barge, and for some time afterward, your boat will be tossed around. Make sure you leave nothing on the table that could fall off.*

'*The canal is poorly equipped for leisure craft. Some quays have been fitted out but they are rare. The banks are hard to reach and there is so much traffic on the water that mooring in the countryside is not recommended. There are a few commercial quays where you can tie up as long as you leave room for any barge which might appear.* '[11]

This was hardly reassuring and this was certainly not a canal we would ever have chosen to use if other options had been open to us. It meant we also had another tunnel to negotiate, the Tunnel de Ruyaulcourt, built below the level of the surrounding water table and just over four kilometres long. All other tunnels that we have come across have worked on an alternating one-way system but this one has the unusual feature of being two-way in the central section. Building an underground structure big enough to fit two of the large commercial barges side by side with room to pass is one of those engineering feats that leave you so in awe of the achievement that you almost forget how a little boat like us will be bounced around in such an enclosed space. There are times when it is best not to think about something until it is right in front of you and this was one of those times.

By now it was early August, with temperatures flitting between 33 to 38 degrees, and we had a decision to make.

---

[11] Source: Editions du Breil – *Guide No 20 Picardie*

Normally, although that is a word we can use less and less these days, our cruising season extends to early September. Given that so many boats were heading to their winter ports early in order to avoid the closures, we had to decide whether to carry on cruising or follow their example.

'I don't want to stop,' I said. 'It's just too soon. Why does every month now have to be a record breaker? What happened to all those years when the weather just ambled along without being so extreme?'

I know people have different views on the impact of climate change but I don't doubt it. There were times when I missed those years of happy ignorance, times when the weather could still be maddening and perverse, but at least you knew where you stood. Extreme weather events were more of a rarity and less of a common occurrence. Something precious has been lost and I don't see how we will ever get it back. If I feel a sense of loss now, I dread to think how I will feel in ten years' time.

In the end we made the decision to err on the side of caution, brave the Canal du Nord and head for our winter mooring. I had assumed that we would spend most of our time in these last few days cruising through an industrial landscape but in fact it was surprisingly rural. The moorings were as expected, generally not places to stay in for more than one night, although we did find a couple of quieter spots and the tunnel was a breeze, mainly because luck was with us and we had it all to ourselves! Timing is all on busy canals – just like the M25 in the good old bad old days. Once through the tunnel our elation quickly evaporated as we ran into a backlog of commercials and spent a cumulative total of two and a half hours tied up at the next six locks waiting for a passage through. You can't win 'em all.

And so our season ended with a whimper rather than a bang. We arrived at our winter port of Valenciennes on 19th August with mixed feelings. There was a sense of relief that we had arrived, but there was also an underlying sadness at how life on the French waterways was changing. There was no doubt it was struggling, seemingly more so each year from our limited experience, but then perhaps the veterans who had been living this life for far longer than we had might argue that fluctuations on this level were normal and that a good year can often follow a bad year.

Whatever the reality, this would be our last cruising season in France for a while. We were now moored up within fifteen kilometres from the border with Belgium and next year, barring unknown catastrophic future events, we planned to cruise through Belgium and into the Netherlands. It was time for a change, to explore different countries and learn different ways of doing things.

Chapter 14

The cost of freedom

❖ ❖ ❖

One of the best things about living on a boat in France is that it can be done with relatively little money. I divide our budget into three sections: what the boat costs us when we are cruising on her, what she costs over the winter and, lastly, an allowance for annual maintenance.

When we are cruising our costs consist of the following elements:

1. The cost of moorings
2. Electricity and water
3. Permit/*vignette*
4. Fuel
5. Insurance

France is one of the best places for cruising not just because of the extensive network of navigable rivers and canals, but also because of the number of moorings. Some are in marinas, both small and large, and it is often the case that the larger the marina, the greater the cost of a mooring for the night or longer. We paid 58€ for one night in Paris but the norm is around 20 to 25€. Prices vary according to the size of your boat.

The real joy of French cruising comes from the rural mooring spots, often with room for only one or two boats, and many of these are free. They provide bollards so that you can tie up securely and, at times, there is even free electricity and water. We have solar panels on board which means we can generate our own electricity. If you do have to pay for it, it is only a few euros for the services and typically 5€ or 10€ for the mooring. We don't know why there is such an abundance of free moorings, but suspect it is due to their supportive attitude towards attracting tourism. Whatever the reason, we are grateful for it and happy to spend our money supporting the local shops in return. Over our most recent five-month summer cruising season we spent 500€ on moorings and that was higher than usual as we had no option but to spend a week in an expensive marina outside Paris while we recovered from Covid.

The French waterways are managed by the VNF (Voie Navigables de France) and they require each boat to buy an annual permit, a *vignette*, which goes towards funding the maintenance of the network. Given the level of service they provide and the cost of keeping the waterways open this is very good value for money. You can pay for a whole year (427€) or for shorter time periods, from a day, a week or a month.

Our boat runs on diesel, although we may dream of an electric boat, and she consumes far more than a car does, not so surprising given that she weighs thirteen tonnes. Consumption figures vary from boat to boat and from year to year, but in 2022 we travelled 900 kilometres between early April to mid-August and spent 640€ on fuel.

The final cost in this section is annual boat insurance which is compulsory and marinas will ask to see proof of it when you book your mooring. We pay around 380€ for a fully comprehensive policy.

The second section of our budget relates to the cost of winter moorings. Some people spend all year on their boats, and indeed so did we for the first year. It's a matter of personal choice, but cruising is limited during the winter as many ports close down, water and electricity are turned off and standing out in the rain getting soaked to the skin as you make your way up or down countless locks isn't much fun. Those who do live on their boats over the winter will usually settle in a port or marina that will allow them to live on board, with electricity and water included in the price. We prefer to spend our winter away from the boat travelling and so our task is simpler. We just need to find a port where we feel *Olivia Rose* will be secure, preferably with somebody around to keep an eye on her until we return in the spring. These winter rates for *hivernage*, as it is called, can vary considerably. In 2022/23 it cost us 819€ for the year at Valenciennes, one of the cheapest places we have come across. More typically it can be in the region of 1,300 to 1,600€. Because of the way that marinas structure their charges it is often cheaper to pay for a year rather than six months at winter rates plus one or two months at full rates, and so we usually end up paying for a full year even though we don't need it. I should clarify that these costs are for inland moorings only. As soon as you head to the coast and the sailing fraternity, prices become considerably higher.

Some marinas require boats to be taken out of the water over the winter and stored on land, usually because there is a danger of flooding, and this incurs the added cost of a crane to lift the boat out at the end of the season and another to put it back in the following spring. Again, costs vary, from between 250€, if you're lucky, up to 650€ if you're not so lucky. And that is just for one lift, so that number will double. We only pick a port where the boat has to come out if we need to do it anyway for maintenance.

Here is a summary of our summer and winter costs for the year from April 2022 to April 2023. This has been a cheaper year than some, as we got a good deal on our winter mooring and have not travelled as far as we have in previous years. Each year is different. All costs are in euros but I have also given the final total in sterling as a comparison.

1.	Mooring costs (summer) water and electricity)	500	(includes
2.	Mooring costs (winter)	819	
3.	Diesel	641	
4.	Insurance	385	
5.	*Vignette*	427	

Total   **2,772€ (£2,453)**

When you consider that figure includes your accommodation and your means of transport for five months, your yearly insurance and permit, you can see why it is such a cheap way of living. However, there is a downside, as you will see from the next section.

The third element of the cost of living on a boat is maintenance and repairs. This is the sting in the tail. Boats take a lot of looking after. Maintaining the paintwork is a never-ending task, and although work above the waterline can be done as you go along in a bid to spread the work out, there will come a time when the boat has to be lifted out, pressure washed, sanded down and painted below the waterline. Woodwork around windows or doors also needs constant care and attention, the engine needs servicing, all the onboard systems such as plumbing and electrics need to be kept in good working order, and rusty patches and leaks dealt with swiftly before a small problem becomes a big one. We do all the painting and general maintenance ourselves as it would cost too much to pay a professional, and Michael also services the engine himself. Often it is hard, uncomfortable work, but it is the only way we can afford to keep the boat going.

On top of the regular maintenance, there are the things that we never saw coming: the unexpected failure of this, that or the other – and there are many of them on a boat. Some items can cost pennies to replace, others quickly reach bills of thousands of pounds, buying a new engine being one particularly soul-destroying example. Our boat cost £50,000 to buy, a modest sum in the world of boating, but even so we have been shocked at how much it has cost us to keep her on the water. We might hope that we have sorted out the major problems and that we are now in a more settled period, but that would be tempting fate. There is a well-known acronym in the boating world that sums up the situation: B.O.A.T standing for 'bring out another thousand'. Each year is different and we have found it impossible to predict what money we will need. We can only sustain this lifestyle because we had a pot of money from our house sale which we could dip into for emergencies, but that pot has now reached a point where there are no spare funds for major problems. *Olivia Rose* has been informed of the situation and told to behave herself. There is no doubt that it's a wonderful life, but it's not for the faint-hearted!

The other half of our year is much cheaper to maintain. Le Shack is an off-grid, tiny home. We generate all our electricity from solar and battery power with a generator as back-up, and heating comes from a woodburner. Insurance and property tax on such a small dwelling are negligible, far less than in the UK. Using house-sitting as a means of travel, effectively bartering our services so that our accommodation is free, means our only outlay is the cost of diesel to get us to the various properties.

A key factor that allows us to live this way is because we are in France, a country where property prices are not prohibitive, where the authorities are open and supportive to off-grid living, and where they have a generous attitude to tourism and travelling. Granted, there have been times when the paperwork has seemed onerous, but I think it's unavoidable in the world we live in today. It would be both more difficult and more expensive to try to live this life in the UK, or at least that is our perception of it.

Chapter 15

Boat-sitting in Belgium

❖ ❖ ❖

We had visited Belgium only once, some years ago, a weekend trip in the camper van to Bruges. A chance encounter now brought us to a city that we had never heard of in a region that we knew nothing about. We had met the owners of this barge as we cruised along the Somme a few months earlier. Now we found ourselves looking after their dog and their barge for a fortnight while it rested at its winter mooring and they visited Spain to see friends.

Because we spend so much of our lives on the move we also spend a great deal of time poring over maps, trying to decide where exactly we should go, and what sights to see. When the whole of Europe is your playground, the sheer number of choices can be overwhelming, and at times I have felt like a young child in a sweet shop, agonising over whether to pick the pear drops or the chocolate peanuts, worrying that I might choose one and then wish I had chosen the other. For this short interlude the destination had been chosen for me and there was a surprising lightness of being that came with it, a relief that the responsibility had been removed. For the next two weeks we would be living on a barge on the River Leie in the town of Kortrijk, in the north west of the country.

The barge was very different to *Olivia Rose*, around twenty metres long, a bigger, heavier boat than we were used to, weighing in at probably sixty tonnes compared to our thirteen. Rather than being moored to the shore by ropes there was a permanent metal gangplank extending out over a metre and a half of water and the mooring had its own gate so that we could lock ourselves in each night. She was a beautifully appointed boat but the best thing were the bookshelves in the main cabin, wall to wall and ceiling to floor. I practically swooned with joy for we have just two tiny bookshelves on *Olivia Rose* and if there is one thing I miss from my past life it is all the hundreds of books that I had collected over so many years. The middle section of this bookcase was a clever *trompe l'oeil*, a panel of books that were in reality a door through to the main sleeping cabin. You would never know it was there as it joined seamlessly to the rest of the bookcase, but it was our own secret passage, and I felt a childlike thrill each time I opened it.

The dog went by the name of Tin-Tin, an endearing and affectionate little man who liked nothing more than to wedge his behind into Michael's chest as we sat out on deck, plonk his two front feet squarely on Michael's knees to give himself some stability and then gaze intently into the distance, canine skipper of the boat.

In times past and future this mooring spot was, and will be, a peaceful oasis in a busy city, but for the time being it had building sites on both banks. Each morning at seven we woke to the sound of the crane, learning to recognise the distinctive whirring noise it made as it powered up. It was barely fifty metres away from us, and had become our new, decidedly unwelcome, alarm clock. Teams of men began work on three different blocks of residential flats whilst it was still half-dark, floodlights fixed to the base of the crane giving a false dawn. Our days were spent listening to a din of banging and grinding, welding and cutting, of cement mixers and blowtorches, of men shouting and the persistent blare of a radio, which surely none of them could hear through their ear defenders. How can the human race make so much noise?

All day long the crane hoisted building materials from the ground up to the roof where most of the work was being done. I screwed my eyes up and tried to see who was in the cabin so high above me, the man in the sky exercising such delicate control, but there was no-one there. Instead it was all controlled by a man on the ground, a remote control device hung around his neck, and he absently twiddled knobs and pushed levers whilst yelling instructions at his fellow workers. If there had ever been some mystery, some wonder at the astonishing power of these other-worldly, towering giants, modern technology had overcome it, made it pedestrian.

As evening fell and the builders went home the normal sounds of the city could be heard: police sirens wailing and church bells tolling, planes droning overhead and the muted sound of the traffic as it crept over the bridge, stalled in the rush hour. The footpath that ran along the waterside was filled with cyclists on their way home and people walking their dogs. At night it was strangely quiet for a city and we were left in peace, just us and the crane, reflected with a mechanical beauty in the still waters.

We picked up a leaflet from the tourist office. It proudly stated that Kortrijk was experiencing a regeneration, a metamorphosis of development and construction that would breathe new life into the city. As I stood on the river bank I counted seven cranes in addition to what had now become 'our' crane. Walking through the old part of the city, past the much-photographed Broel Towers, window-shopping my way past designer clothes boutiques, I was struck by the number of blocks of flats in various stages of development. Some were newly finished, and through the plate glass frontages I could see that most of them were empty, unfurnished. Who was going to buy these flats? Where was this great influx of people coming from? It is the curse of the constant traveller to ask questions and not be around long enough to find out the answers.

❖ ❖ ❖

Kortrijk was a city for cyclists. Hardly anyone wore helmets and they all travelled at speed. The racing bikes and their lycra-clad riders were a minority, outnumbered by children riding to school, by adults cycling to work or to the shops, and the preferred design of bike was the sit-up-and-beg variety, rather than the hunched forward and down position beloved by the racers. As in so much of Europe, the bikes ruled the road: the cars were expected to give way and pedestrians needed eyes in the back of their heads to avoid being run over. As the schools emptied we would see a mother with what can best be described as a deep wheelbarrow attached to the extended front wheel of her bike with two children bouncing around inside it. On several occasions I spotted a man with a wheelchair attached to the front of his bike and a young child firmly strapped in, his back slightly crooked, his shoulders set at an unnatural angle, leaning into the corners and grinning madly with joy as they sped with no thought of safety along the river trail. I had no idea whether it was his son, or whether he was a carer who offered this service, but my heart lifted to see them. What a wonderful gift to be able to give to someone whose mobility was severely impaired.

Our hosts had kindly offered us the use of their electric bikes and we plotted a route that would take us out of the city.

'You look very strange,' laughed Michael as I sat on this strange bike, my knees coming high as I pedalled, my back straight, so different to the position I was used to.

'I think I quite like it,' I said as I wobbled my way off down the path. 'Although I'm not sure what my knees are going to make of it.'

We followed the river north out of the city, past never-ending, sprawling industrial sites and factories, guessing at what they manufactured from the smells that wafted across the cycle trail, hints of fertiliser, of malt and grain, and the unmistakable cloying stench of a sewage plant. At last the industrial landscape thinned and eventually disappeared and we saw farmhouses and green fields. I stopped at one point and sniffed the air.

'I can smell sprouts.'

Indeed we were surrounded by them, lush and green and pungent, conjuring immediate memories of Christmas turkey with all the trimmings. The next farmhouse had an honesty stall by the gate, leeks and cabbages piled up on a table, freshly picked from the surrounding fields.

'We need two euros,' said Michael, picking up a bunch of long, thick, juicy leeks, five of them, perfect for a leek and potato soup.

'I didn't bring a purse,' I said.

He rummaged around in his pockets and found some loose change. We strapped a bunch to the pannier racks on the back of his bike and I was treated to the aroma of fresh leeks as I cycled behind him until, all too soon, we were back in the city once more and I was breathing in car fumes instead of an earthy vegetable.

❖ ❖ ❖

We drove out for a day trip to Ypres, although perhaps 'day trip' is the wrong term, conjuring up an image of a happy-go-lucky sort of day rather than a sombre visit to pay our respects to those who lost their lives in the carnage of The Great War. We visited the Menin Gate Memorial to the Missing, which lists the names of more than 54,000 officers and men who have no known graves. The Flanders Fields Museum documents the history of the war in Belgium, the strategies, the numbers of lives lost in each battle as a few metres of ground were gained and then lost again. As with so many museums these days it was an interactive experience, with handsets to hold and sensors to activate. With my handset held close to my ear I listened as a modern-day professor of history explained that the ratio of dead to injured, across all wars not just this one, tended to be one to four. Ten million died in this war and if he is right that means forty million were injured, many of them serious injuries with limbs lost, injuries that would blight the rest of their lives.

There were stories that seemed missing from this place, although I am sure they are well documented elsewhere. We all know that the men who survived this war came back changed, unable to talk about what they had experienced, struggling to find their place in society. The doctors and nurses who tended the sick and the dying experienced their own trauma, no less horrific, but who tells their story? And then there are the animals who also played their part and paid dearly for it. An estimated eight million horses, donkeys and mules died within those four years, a figure not much less than the human toll.

Glass cabinets displayed a diverse collection of war memorabilia: military uniforms, hideous examples of gas masks, even a mock-up of a typical trench. Information boards showed pictures of cities bombed to rubble, Ypres being one of them, and black and white photos of refugees fleeing from their homes to avoid both the bombings and the forced deportations of civilians, swallowed up by a war-mongering neighbour, perhaps never to see their own country again. Similar images from Ukraine now filled our own newspapers, suggesting that nothing changes. The majority of humans have no interest in war, would rather live in peace than fight, but still the men in power grow greedy for more land, or fall prey to paranoia, fearing that their power is threatened and so history repeats and repeats itself.

I could feel myself sliding into a miserable despair and it was a relief when the exit turnstiles appeared and I could drop my handset into the box and leave. I took a deep breath of fresh air, grateful for this reconstructed city, thankful for our modern reality and a life where I felt safe.

❖ ❖ ❖

Despite being a small country, Belgium has three official languages and many sub-dialects within those main categories. This can be a minefield for the foreign visitor as the two main regions of the country don't appreciate it if, in a moment of understandable confusion, you use the wrong language.

Almost 60 per cent of people speak Dutch, most of them living to the north in Flanders and sharing a border with the Netherlands. The Belgium version of the Dutch language is similar but not the same as that spoken by a Dutch person, primarily in that the accent and some of the vocabulary is different. It is also referred to as 'Flemish' although this isn't officially recognised as a language.

Almost 40 per cent of people speak French, living to the south in Wallonia and sharing a border with France. Just under one per cent speak German, and they live primarily in Liège on the eastern border with Germany.

'How am I supposed to remember all that?' asked Michael.

'Think of the language of the country that they share a border with and then you'll be ok. Although Brussels has its own rules. It's in the north, in Flanders, and so should be Dutch speaking, but as it is the capital it's supposed to be bilingual in French and Dutch. In reality they speak more French, which makes no sense.'

'I assume down south we speak French but what do we speak up here then?'

'Apparently English is your safest bet, as it's accepted that not that many people speak Dutch. But don't speak French. It doesn't go down well.'

'You'll be popular then.'

This was said with some irony. French is the only foreign language that I can speak. We can be in Spain, Italy, or indeed any non-English-speaking country in the world and yet as soon as I open my mouth, it is French that comes out. It seems to be my default setting after English and not something I have any control over. I am aware that it is ridiculous and, in this case, might cause offence but I can't help it.

'You'll have to do all the talking,' I said.

Michael's answer was to raise a disbelieving eyebrow.

We went out several times a day to give Tin-Tin a chance to

stretch his legs and do his ablutions. Walking anywhere in France, particularly with a dog, is often a sociable experience, with passers-by wishing you '*Bonjour*' and often stopping to admire and pet the dog. We wanted to be able to respond in like fashion whilst in Belgium and so had learnt the Dutch equivalent of 'Good morning', which was '*Goedendag*'.

'Have you noticed something strange?' I said.

'Yes,' said Michael. 'This dog has cocked his leg at least ten times in the two hundred yards. Quite astonishing. There can't be anything left to pee surely.'

'Not that,' I said, although it was true that Tin-Tin was assiduous in marking his territory. Having only ever had female dogs, we had been slightly taken aback. 'Have you noticed that nobody looks us in the eye? Nobody says hello.'

We walked on into town, both of us now obsessively noting whether anyone would smile or say good morning.

'Perhaps it's because it's a town. They might be more friendly in a village.'

'It wouldn't stop them in France. They can't help themselves.'

I left Michael and Tin-Tin outside the bakery and joined the small queue inside the shop. In France, a queue is an opportunity for an outpouring of greetings, with '*Bonjours*' shared on the way in and on the way out, regardless of the fact that most of the people are likely to be complete strangers. It had seemed excessive when we first moved to the country but we had become used to it and as I stood in that strangely silent queue in the bakery in Kortrijk I realised I missed it.

As we walked back I made a determined effort to smile and say '*Goedendag*' to everybody we passed. Some people nodded curtly, some people smiled back and some ignored me completely.

'It's not France, is it?' I said as we arrived back at the boat, although I don't know why I was surprised.

Europe is not one homogenous mass. Each country is different and the amount of time that we had spent in Belgium was far too short to make assumptions about the friendliness of the nation. What was more interesting was the fact that we were using France as our benchmark, not the UK. It was another sign of how our sense of where we now belonged was changing and, perhaps, we were becoming a little more French in our habits.

Chapter 16

Finding answers in the silence

❖ ❖ ❖

The Eglise Notre Dame de la Gorge was too small to merit the description of a church. Looking at it from the outside it was more like the simplest of chapels, a rather plain building situated on the winding mountain road that led out along the Monjoie valley from St-Gervais-les-Bains in the French Alps. We were staying in the town on a house-sit of four days, our short-term home a traditional wooden chalet where we were responsible for a dog called Filou, which means 'rascal' in French. Thankfully he didn't live up to his name but was charming and friendly. Nestling on a grassy plain by the river, with the mountains rising up behind it, the chapel marked the end of the road. As I climbed the short flight of steps up to it I noticed that the door didn't sit snugly in the frame and light from inside the building was shining, miracle-like, through the gaps. It was barely above freezing after a sharp frost the night before, but it felt colder as the building was still in the shade. I suspected it wouldn't feel any warmer inside and pulled my coat tight around me as I pushed the door open.

I am not a religious person and yet, like so many people, I am drawn to churches. I have never been able to explain this fascination to myself. I am content in my state of non-belief and don't feel the need to search for a connection with a deity who will give my life meaning or make my passing, hopefully a distant event, less of a trial. I have explored all manner of churches and part of the attraction is the architectural ambition, the grandeur of the building as a feat of construction. Allowing myself to indulge in a whimsical game of make-believe, I like to imagine that the god of the great cathedrals, with their soaring arches and magnificent windows, would be equally grand, looking down on his chosen few with remote haughtiness. As I stepped inside this little chapel on a cold November morning, I thought that this god might be more approachable. It was surprisingly warm, and the light was soft. This had been the local parish church for the residents of the valley since the thirteenth century and was in surprisingly good condition. The ceiling was painted a pale honey colour and, whilst the exterior had been simple, the altar was a little gaudy, statues of Our Lady perched in guilt-edged alcoves, with cherubs and crowns as ornaments, and Jesus hanging on the cross as the centre piece.

There was no-one else there but me and so I sat down on a wooden pew and wondered who else had sat in this same spot. How many people had lived in this remote valley all those years ago? Did they come to church out of duty and tradition or from conviction? I pictured the priest standing behind the simple table and speculated as to what subjects he chose for his sermons and whether they were any different to those that might be chosen today. As our sins don't change greatly, I imagine there would still be a common relevant link.

Eventually I heard the door creak open behind me and a whisper of glacial air brushed my cheeks. There was the sound of footsteps on the flagstones and low murmurs in French. I turned to find a group of six people crowding in through the doorway. The spell was broken. It was time for me to leave. Crossing over the river, I took the steep, stony track that led up to the Pont de la Téna, an ancient Roman stone bridge, picking my way carefully as the trail was slippery from recent rainfall.

Halfway up the track there was a bench and I sat down, leant back on it, closed my eyes and listened. I could hear the cawing of crows, and the occasional flap of their wings in the branches of the pine trees. That was all. When I opened my eyes again the mountains seemed larger than they had a moment before, lofty and remote, reaching greedily to fill all the empty spaces and forcing the sky to recede. I am not used to mountains on this scale and they take me out of my comfort zone. We humans turn to religion for many reasons, with the need to feel a sense of awe, of respect, of love for something bigger than ourselves. On days when we wonder what the point of our day-to-day lives is, particularly in difficult times, we might look to religion to give us an answer to help us carry on.

I have never experienced that connection or found any answers within a church, but I did find both on that day, sitting alone on a bench in the high mountains. It has happened before, on other days when I have been out alone in the wild places. I wouldn't call it an alternative religion, in truth I am not sure what to call it, but it is a connection that comes from the mountains and forests, from the water and the high open spaces, places where nature is so strong and intense that it feels like a living being. When I question what the point of humanity is in general and me in particular, this is where I find answers. The reply comes through the silence, suggesting that it is enough to exist, to just be, and not to look for more.

Chapter 17

Chamonix – closed for business

❖ ❖ ❖

'*Madame, je suis désolée mais il est fermé,*' said the lady in the tourist office in Chamonix. 'In fact, everything is closed. The cable car to the Aiguille du Midi, the Montenvers Railway and many of the restaurants in the town. In November we are between seasons and this is when maintenance is done or the local business owners take a holiday. By the middle of December everything will be open again.'

I looked at her in despair. We wouldn't be here in the middle of December. We were only here for a few days. I had visited Chamonix once before, when I was seventeen and the French family that I was staying with as part of a language exchange had brought me with them on their annual summer holiday. We had squeezed ourselves into a tiny flat in nearby Les Houches and I had fond memories of taking the cable car and also of standing on the glacier. These few days were supposed to have been a trip down memory lane but it appeared we had picked the wrong month to visit.

I explained to the woman behind the desk that I had been here 45 years ago, at which point my hand came out, of its own volition, to indicate a child of about five years old, rather than the teenager I had been. I have no idea why I did that, but I suspect my subconscious was in denial at the sudden realisation that I had somehow reached an age where my teenage memories were 45 years old.

'*Dites-moi, Madame*,' I said, moving hastily on before she had time to work out the maths, 'I remember visiting the Mer de Glace but I have heard that much of it has disappeared now due to climate change. Is this so?'

'*Ah mais oui, c'est triste*,' was all she had to say to my question, although she didn't look sad. 'But you must come back another time. Everything has changed since all those years ago that you were here and there is much more to see at the top when you take the cable car.' She pulled out a brochure. 'You would enjoy this. We call it "the glass box" because it is glazed on all sides, even under your feet. As you look down there is a drop of 1,000 metres. Impressive, don't you think?'

We agreed it was impressive and left, wandering around a town that had grown beyond all recognition. Many shops were indeed shut and it felt like a town-in-waiting, rather drab on a grey winter's day. I knew it would look and feel very different once the winter season started and holidaymakers filled the streets, although we later learnt that the usual opening of the ski season has been delayed in parts of the mountains due to a lack of snow.

The Mer de Glace, which means the Sea of Ice, is France's longest glacier. I have an old photo of my younger self standing on it in the August sunshine in 1977, the snow pristine and blindingly white, but those days are long gone. Glaciers grow during the winter and shrink during the summer, a normal and natural cycle which only works if the climate is stable. Over the past decades the scales have tipped in the wrong direction and that natural balance has been overturned by a warming climate. The once-beautiful Sea of Ice is dying, one of 500 glaciers in the Alps that are suffering the same fate and receding further each year. Geologists at the Federal Institute of Technology in Zurich predict that half of all alpine glaciers will be gone by 2050, and that most of those that remain will disappear by the turn of the century.

This will have an obvious effect on tourism, but the consequences are more far-reaching than that. The meltwater from glaciers is dammed and has long been used by local communities and farmers but it also generates green energy through hydro stations. There are 500 of these hydro plants across the Alps and their future, and the contribution they make towards a sustainable energy source, is now in question. Another problem arises as the snow melts and the rock face becomes increasingly unstable and dangerous. Reports of rockfalls killing people and livestock, blocking streets and damaging buildings are now a regular feature of life for those who live in the shadow of the glaciers. Perhaps the most sobering thought of all is that much of the damage has now been done and the consequences cannot be reversed or stopped, even if we somehow, impossibly, halted all carbon emissions tomorrow.[12]

Climate change is now part of our vocabulary, a looming disaster that we are all aware of, and yet for many of us it is still just words. It is too large a disaster to comprehend and yet here in the Alps there is a tangible proof of how a change in climate can ravage the land. The first sign that something is wrong comes from the colour. That pure white that is imprinted on my mind has gone. Even driving along the valley, peering up at what remains of the glacier, I can see it is a dirty grey colour, so very different to my memory, so diminished. Dust from the falling rocks and loose debris scattered over the surface has aged it in

---

[12] Source: stories.cgtneurope.tv, 'The Alps – the death of ice', 28th August 2021, Elizabeth Mearns and Ross Cullen

the same way that we humans age, our skin becoming sallow and sunken as the bloom of youth deserts us. The other sign that this glacier is in its death throes is the obvious, measurable limits of where it once was and where it is now. In 1988, when a new cable car was inaugurated to give better access, tourists had only to take three steps to reach the ice. By around 2017 they needed to take 430 steps, with a prediction that 20 steps would need to be added each year to keep pace with the reduction in size.[13]

I felt sad that we had not been able to take the cable car and scare ourselves silly standing in the glass box, sad that we had not been able to visit the Mer de Glace before it shrunk even more. And yet a small part of me was relieved. I still had that old picture of a young girl in shorts, feet akimbo on the snow, grinning in delight. At least I saw it in its glory days and I can hang on to those memories. They say you should never go back. In this case, perhaps they are right.

---

[13] Source: United Nations Environment Programme, www.unep.org, 'On thin, melting ice', 6th September 2018

Chapter 18

If a fence can't hold water,
it can't hold a goat

❖ ❖ ❖

We left St Gervais in torrential rain, the peaks lost in the clouds, the valley a lesser place without their brooding presence, a soulless corridor of factories, offices and out-of-town retail parks that could have been anywhere. As we drove north towards Lac Léman the terrain changed subtly, the green-black of the evergreen conifers lightened by gold and bronze and the slopes carpeted with beech leaves, the contrasting colours made richer by the rain. The industrial and commercial landscape petered out, replaced by wooden chalets and fields and a welcome sense of space. We climbed the last few miles to our destination out of a valley wreathed in mist, grabbed a single bag from the van and ran for the front door, soaked in seconds.

Our English hosts, who had moved to this area six months ago, welcomed us with a cup of tea, and introduced us to the two kittens, four ducks, three chickens and three guinea fowl that would be our company for the next two and a half weeks. They explained that goats from a neighbouring farm had been getting into the garden, but they had spoken to the farmer and asked him to fix the fencing so that it would not be a problem whilst they were away. They'd left us his telephone number just in case.

It is customary to share a meal on the eve of a house-sit, a good time to run through how everything works. Sometimes conversation is stilted but other times, as it did on that night, it can feel as if we have known these strangers all our lives. This is when house-sitting becomes more than just having a place to stay. It opens a window onto other people's lives, allowing us to hear about their past and to share their experience of living in a foreign country. There is always much to learn, to commiserate or laugh about, to be inspired by. Our hosts would be leaving at 3am the following morning and we would be leaving a few hours before they arrived back at the end of the house-sit so it was likely that, after tonight, we would never see them again. I relish these brief encounters where there is no time to take anything for granted, where each moment should be enjoyed to the full.

We woke the next morning to the clanging of goat bells. I pulled open the curtains of the main living room and found myself face to face with a large nanny goat. We stared at each other for a second or two, me bleary-eyed with sleep, she munching on a twig she'd stripped from the buddleia next to the door, and then I banged on the window. She thought about it for a second and then ambled off, quite unconcerned. She wasn't alone. There were around fifteen of them, a mixture of mature females and young kids, and they were destroying the garden with impressive and slightly manic efficiency. One had its head buried in the compost bin, another was nosing through fallen apples, another stripping the leaves from the raspberry canes. They had already consumed the broccoli and cabbage on a previous visit before we arrived but a small group of them had jumped up into the vegetable beds and were finishing off what little remained. We threw on some clothes and chased them off but once we walked around the perimeter we could see that they'd be back in no time. The electric fencing was down in numerous places and had shorted out. Animals have an uncanny knack of sensing when this happens and always take advantage of it. I rang the owner and told them and then I rang the farmer.

He turned up two days later and by chance I spotted him walking up the track.

'*Bonjour monsieur,*' I said, waddling up behind him in a pair of borrowed wellie boots that were three sizes too big for me. 'Are these your goats?'

'*Mais oui.*' He looked at me but didn't smile.

I introduced myself and explained that the goats had broken

into the garden again.

'*Mais ce n'est pas grave.*' He shrugged. '*C'est la campagne.*'

I thought about saying that this was indeed the countryside but that didn't mean it was okay for him to let his animals wander wherever they wanted, but then thought better of it. This wasn't my fight; all we wanted was for the fencing to be fixed. He then went on to say that if people were going to get upset about things like this then they should have bought a house down in the town. I thanked him for fixing the fencing and left it at that. This was a familiar story, townspeople and country people having conflicting perspectives on boundaries, a difference which only becomes more complex when you add in the element of newcomer versus someone born to the area. We had experienced this ourselves in our smallholding days and there was no reason for it to be any different in another country. It was a human condition and we fall victim to the same prejudices regardless of which country we live in.

As we walked back down the track the farmer stopped and gestured at the chickens.

'These are fine birds. But beware of the fox. There are plenty of them here and they will come in the night.' He said the next words slowly, as if to a child. 'You must take care and shut the birds away at dusk or you will lose them.'

I could have told him that I'd kept chickens for years and

knew perfectly well how to look after them but yet again I held my tongue, not sure whether I was doing it due to an ingrained, and at times annoying, habit of British politeness or because I didn't know how a French person would have reacted in such a situation. On the one hand, the French are very polite and there are strict rules to adhere to, but on the other hand they can also be blunt to the point of rudeness. As always in these situations I erred on the side of caution and avoided a confrontation. This wasn't my house and it would do no good to make things more difficult.

The farmer might have mended the electric fencing but the goats paid no heed. To begin with we tried to chase them off but it was pointless as they came and went as they pleased, ducking under or jumping over or barging through as the fancy took them. At one point I went out there with my walking stick, determined to herd them back onto their own field, but was seen off by one of the lead nanny goats. I stared at her and she stared at me, eyes bulging, obviously confident that in a staring competition she would win hands down. When I didn't retreat she stamped a foot and started to walk towards me, lowering her head and those impressive horns in a threatening manner. I have been headbutted by a much smaller goat in the past and had the bruises for days so, shame-faced, I conceded defeat. I had always thought that goats had no facial expression until that day. Now I know that they can smirk as well as anyone.

During the summer months these goats had been looked after by a goatherd, who milked them twice a day and took them up into the mountains and forests to keep them cool in the heat. He would bring them back down each night and put them in the barn. This regime lasted for six months and, whilst he was paid for his labour, it was not a lot of money. During the winter he would have to find another job to tide him over. Our goatherd obviously enjoyed his job, and had a better relationship with them than we did, as he hoped next year to work in an *alpage*, or mountain pasture, on a full-time basis. As for the goats, they spend most of the winter indoors and indeed a few days after we left we heard that they were all safely installed in the barn and no longer running rampant. They are not milked during this time, which sends the signal to their bodies to come into oestrus, and they are put to the billy goat. The pregnancy lasts around 150 days and then the milking season begins again.

When we had our smallholding in Wales I always wanted to keep goats. We didn't have sufficient land at the time and so we never went down that road. There is no doubt they are appealing, particularly the kids, but having seen how difficult it is to keep them contained I think I am cured of that particular longing. There is an old saying that 'If a fence can't hold water, it can't hold goats' and now I know how true that is.[14]

---

[14] Source: http://www.theprairiehomestead.com

Chapter 19

Coming home

❖ ❖ ❖

'Credit where credit is due,' I said as I hoovered up a pile of mouse droppings from the food cupboards. 'Mice are very good at what they do.'

'If by that you mean eating everything that crosses their path and then pooing on it, I suppose you're right.' Michael held up a roll of bin liners, now consisting more of holes than plastic. 'I don't think it's anything to be particularly proud of.'

I've always had a soft spot for mice. It doesn't extend to allowing them access to our food, but there is something appealing about them despite the damage they do. I admire their diligence and determination. Before we left back in April I had removed anything that I thought would attract the mice, leaving only a few tinned foods and jars in the store cupboard. However I had missed a carton of tomato passata, which was now an empty husk of its former self, a hole nibbled in the bottom of it and the contents presumably consumed as it drained out. A bar of soap by the kitchen sink had disappeared completely, but they had gifted us a large pile of droppings in the soap dish in exchange. There is nothing good to be said about mouse poo other than that it acts as a clear sign of where they have been.

It was midday in late November and we had just arrived back at Le Shack after an absence of eight months, bar one quick visit back for a couple of dental appointments in early summer. We had braced ourselves for a leaking roof or having to get the shears out to hack our way through the wilderness to the front door but, apart from the mice visitation, all seemed to be fine. For most people returning to their home after time away, it is a simple matter to flick on a light switch and turn on the central heating. As we live off-grid it's not quite so simple for us. The first job is to check the voltage on the batteries and, assuming that they haven't completely drained themselves down on a whim while we've been away, reconnect them to the system. The second job is to reconnect the battery in the generator, fill it up with fresh fuel and then run it for a while to top the batteries up to full. By this stage we now have power and so we can flick the light switches with the best of them. The third, and final, element is to bring the solar panels out of the cabin, where we store them for safe-keeping while we are away, prop them up on their stand in the field and connect them into the system. It was a grey and drizzly afternoon when we arrived, but we were expecting sunshine in the morning and so they would be in place and ready to capture our free power supply by lunchtime, which is when the winter sun crests the ridge and floods the field with light.

It took a matter of minutes to bring in some logs and kindling and get the woodburner going and a few more to plug the gas canister into the camping stove so that we had heat to cook on. We obtain our water from the grid, so that was easy, a simple matter of turning a stopcock. Last but not least was the composting loo.

'Why is the loo always my job?' I grabbed the broom, ready to do battle with the spider population lurking in the rafters of our outside loo-with-a-view.

'Probably because that sort of thing is women's work?' suggested Michael, who likes to live dangerously every now and then.

For peace of mind when visiting the loo a thorough de-cobwebbing of the area is essential. The spiders have long coveted this particular space and I don't blame them as it's a pleasing building. It was used by the previous owner as a summer kitchen and must have been a relatively recent addition as both the roof tiles and timbers still look new. Whenever people move into a new home they like to redo everything that was done before in order to make it feel like their own space, and we are no different. We had left the outside tap and sink where they were because the cats, who came with the property, made it clear from the day we moved in that this was their domain. It is one of their favourite places, offering a cool, shady spot in summer, perfect for a full-body stretch across the drainer for maximum relief or to curl up in the sink bowl itself if a more cosy bed is required. There are some battles that you know you will never win, particularly with cats, however we had staked our own claim to the other half of the kitchen. We built a partition wall to section off our new loo area and constructed a wooden frame to support the loo seat, fitting it with a removable front which allowed us to slide a bucket in and out below it.

When we are not there to disturb them the spiders weave their webs in the cavity underneath the seat, as well as overhead in the roof timbers, but after five minutes of vigorous work with the broom it all looked far more inviting. I had cleaned and stacked our bins under the sink before we left, so all that was needed was to remove a dead mouse that had climbed in and not been able to get out again (not the most glamorous of deaths), slide the bucket under the seat and sprinkle a scoop of shavings into the bottom of it. The loo was now ready for business. We had installed a roller blind for privacy, but we've never used it as it blocks a good view up the hill when one is seated. We live in a field in the middle of nowhere and there are no footpaths across our land. The only person who might trespass would be one of the hunt, and my view is that if they want to come where they are not welcome and therefore have to endure the sight of a woman sitting on her own loo in her own field then so be it. It will probably upset them more than it does me.

By the evening the cabin was clean, warm and most things had been packed away. I sat in front of the fire and let my eyes wander round the room. A selection of Michael's framed drawings hung above the sink. They were some of his early sketches, drawn when we were under lockdown: a woodpecker and a kestrel, a wild boar and a squirrel. There was a small bookshelf by my side of the bed, built by Michael from offcuts, and my newest books had been neatly slotted into the last available space. We had closed the curtains against the blackness of the night and they always drew my eye. They were full length, a colourful patchwork, hand-sewn and given as a gift by Michael's mother, and every time I looked at them I would see a different pattern.

Each winter when we return to Le Shack I worry a little that the magic might fade. I wonder if the fact that we are now spending so much time house-sitting, often in large properties with all modern conveniences, might make it hard to be content in this simple abode or that the off-grid nature of our life here might become onerous, too much of a challenge. I question whether you can really call a place home when you spend so little time in it. Now that we are not forced to stay here under a lockdown regime we have been able to travel as we always wanted to, but it means that, for the whole of 2022, we will have been here for slightly less than three months.

As I sat in front of the fire on our first night back I knew that the magic was as strong as it had ever been and, even though we have not spent a great deal of time here this year, there is no doubt that this is home. *Olivia Rose* is also our home and I don't feel the need to place one above the other, but just to accept that they are different, both precious in their own ways. Part of the reason that we are content here is because we have our own things around us, but equally important are the gifts from those we hold dear, thoughtful touches that bring our family close despite the distance and help to make the cabin a warm and welcoming space. The simplicity of the life here is without doubt challenging at times but it is a challenge we enjoy and would hate to give up.

However, the appeal of this place is more than just what we can see, or hear or touch. It has a spirit of its own, offering an oasis of calm in a manic world. Each autumn the leaves fall and each spring the trees grow green yet again and there is a sense of continuity, a stability, an assumption that this wild, beautiful and natural environment will endure. We individual humans come and go and the odds are that our time is running out, but the land is everlasting, even though the climate may cause it to change in form. In a world which seems inherently unstable on so many fronts at the moment, this solid and steady presence is a comfort.

We went to bed that night and fell straight into a deep and peaceful slumber. At four in the morning a loud crunching noise woke us up.

'It's that bloody mouse.' I sat up in bed and fumbled for the light switch. 'It's under the sink.'

'Can't we ignore it?' Michael pulled the covers over his head. 'The mouse trap will get it soon.'

'I need to know what it's eating.' I pulled on my dressing gown, grabbed the torch and gently pulled back the curtain that covered up the under-sink cupboard. 'Ha, thought so. It's in here and it's after my daffodil bulbs.'

I pulled out a plastic carrier bag containing two small sacks of bulbs that were due to be planted in the morning. As I peered inside I caught a glimpse of brown fur.

'It's still in the bag!'

I carried it carefully outside, gripping the top edges closely together, put it sideways on the ground, slid the bags of bulbs out and waited for the mouse to scarper. Nothing happened. I gingerly righted the bag, thinking it must have got away without me seeing it, and as I did so the smallest of mice launched itself into the air in a blind panic, narrowly missing hitting me in the face, and disappeared behind the wood store.

I went back to bed but five minutes later the light was back on again.

'What now?' groaned Michael.

'There's another one, but it's in the kitchen cupboard this time. How can you not hear these things?'

I got down on my hands and knees and shone a torch on the mouse trap. 'He's eaten the peanut butter off the trap without setting it off.'

'Impossible.'

The prospect of his reputation as chief pest controller being called into question was enough to finally get Michael out of bed. The trap was reset, with the bait being pushed more firmly into its little hole, and we went back to bed.

'Can you sleep?'

'Not now I can't.'

'Want to know some interesting mouse facts?' I asked.

'Not really.'

'They have collapsible ribcages. Their ribs bend and contort which is why they can get through such small holes. The biggest part of their body is their head, so if that gets through, then so can the rest of them.'

There was no response to this fascinating piece of information so I tried another tack.

'They can produce between forty to fifty droppings a day. And they constantly give off droplets of urine on the move throughout the day...'

'That is disgusting.'

'But they never need to stop and pee, very efficient. Also they carry some nasty germs, very unhygienic.'

'Have you anything good to say about them?'

'A group of mice is called a "mischief". I think that's rather sweet.'

Eventually I ran out of mouse trivia and the cabin fell silent. Before long, we heard the unmistakable sound of something being shredded.

'How does he manage to make so much noise?' I whispered.

'It's an "it", not a "he". You'll be wanting to give it a name next.'

'That would be silly.'

There was a loud snapping noise, a few distressing thuds as

the mouse twitched violently and then silence. The mouse trap had done its work. And, finally, we managed to get some sleep.

We had inherited two cats with the property but like many half-wild cats in France they had a number of part-time homes, taking food wherever it was offered. Given the fact that we were hardly ever there it gave us peace of mind to know someone would keep an eye on them. Within a few days of us coming back they would eventually turn up, but each time I wondered if it would be the last and that eventually they would move on permanently.

One of the cats, half-black and half-white with a black spot on her rump, spent most of her time down at the organic vegetable farm on the valley floor below us. We called her Spot, for obvious reasons, and they called her Moit-moit, which is French for half-and-half, for equally obvious reasons. On Friday afternoon I made my usual trip down to pick up a veggie box and saw Spot sitting in the yard.

'Hello little one.' I walked over, glad to see her, but she turned her back on me and walked off. The relationship was over.

Our other cat, a little black one, had been adopted by our nearest neighbours and had not come back the last time we were home. After such a long absence this time, we didn't really expect to see her and indeed we didn't. I could see that it was for the best but I missed them.

Chapter 20

Beware the reaper

❖ ❖ ❖

We had travelled back from the UK with a new addition to our armoury in the never-ending war against bracken and brambles in our field – a scythe, a full-size, double- handed tool, with a blade so sharp that it demanded respect and concentration when using it. It was also our only tool as our strimmer had finally admitted defeat earlier in the year and was now consigned to the back of the shed, beyond repair despite numerous efforts.

You might be forgiven for thinking that scything is a simple skill to pick up but it's not and so, during our last trip back to the UK, we booked ourselves onto a scything course.

Scything has its own vocabulary, some of it practical, some of it rooted in old languages, not surprising as this is an ancient art. The handle, which is comprised of a long shaft made of wood fitted with two handgrips, is called a 'snath', a word which comes from Old Norse 'sneitha' meaning to cut. Words more commonly associated with the anatomy of living creatures have been borrowed to pinpoint specific parts of the blade, for example rib, toe, belly, and heel. The size and shape of the blade will depend on the type of work it will do and there are several hundred to choose from.[15]

It immediately became clear that it wasn't a case of picking up any old scythe and wading in. The length of the wooden handle and its grips should be adjusted to fit your height and the blade will be chosen to suit the type of work you will be doing, which may necessitate having a collection of blades. There is a charming adage that states 'You'd no sooner lend someone your scythe than lend them your false teeth', which suggests that scything is primarily the province of the older generation, but today younger men and women are showing an increasing interest in the subject.

We began our morning of instruction by picking out a snath of the right height for each of us, attaching the handles and then the blade.

'Hold the scythe as if you're about to mow, upper grip in your left hand, the lower grip in your right and the blade on your floor to the right,' said our instructor, Andi Rickard, owner of the

---

[15] Source: *Learn to Scythe*, Steve Tomlin

Somerset Scythe School, demonstrating with her own scythe. 'Your right arm will be almost straight and your left arm bent.'

I duly copied her and waited for the next instructions. There was a pause.

'The blade should be on the floor to your right,' she repeated, looking at me. 'Not to your left.'

'Oops.' As a child I had always had a problem differentiating left from right but I thought I had mastered my confusion long ago. Obviously I was wrong.

Out in the field we began practising our technique, drawing an arc from three to eleven o'clock and moving slowly forward, one foot at a time.

'This should be a relaxed, fluid movement,' Andi explained. 'You're looking for the "sweet spot" where the blade stays in contact with the ground at all times. With practice you won't need to concentrate on it, it will come naturally.'

And after a few false starts, it did indeed begin to feel natural, as if the blade were an extension of my body.

'Well done.' She looked surprised, no doubt wrong-footed by my initial confusion of a simple matter of left and right. 'You picked that up quickly.'

I was surprised too, but the action of rolling onto the balls of your toes on one foot and then the other and twisting at the same time was, by pure chance, a yoga movement and so it felt like an old friend rather than something new to learn.

'Now you've got an idea of how to mow, we need to look at sharpening. A blunt blade is no good to anyone and you'll need to recognise the point where it will need honing.'

And so began another new learning curve. By lunchtime we were brain-dead, unable to take in any more information, but we were also the proud owners of our own scythe. We would share it, as we could alter the settings to fit the slight difference in our heights, which went against the advice of the old adage. We wouldn't dream of sharing our false teeth, when and if we ever get to the point of needing them, but our budget didn't allow for having one scythe each. Sometimes you have to break the rules.

We weren't the only people interested in learning how to do things the old-fashioned way. Many of Andi's courses were fully booked and there was a thriving community of people worldwide committed to keeping these skills alive. In the UK the annual West Country Scythe Festival takes place on two days each year in June. It's been going for sixteen years and is the biggest in the country, with competitions, courses and scything products on sale. The 'scythe v strimmer' contest has become quite well known, with the scythe often outperforming the strimmer. Competitions have been held in Europe for decades and are taken very seriously. Only the best teams and individuals can compete here.

The scythe also plays a part in myths and legends, the most infamous being the Grim Reaper, swathed in his black cloak with his scythe over his shoulder, ready to reap the souls of the dead as they journey into the afterlife. It is understandable that people have wished to put a human face on the concept of death over the ages and in earlier times that face had a far friendlier countenance. In Greek mythology a pleasant and helpful young god called Thanatos delivered the souls of the dead to Charon, the ferryman on the River Styx, from where they would enter Hades.

In Norse mythology, the Valkyries, beautiful young women, served as escorts to the souls of warriors who died on the battlefield, helping them on their way to Odin and his 'hall of the slain', Valhalla. Even animals can act as companions, with owls, sparrows and crows being common examples. All these different manifestations are called 'psychopomps', a surprisingly modern-sounding term derived from the ancient Greek word meaning 'the guide of souls'.

It was the plague of the late fourteenth century that changed the tone so dramatically. Twenty-five million people died in the initial outbreak, followed by millions more as the disease continued to flare up for years afterwards. This was a terrible, fearful way to die and it changed how people viewed and responded to death. This period in our history was the birthplace of death being represented as a skeleton, hideous and threatening, often portrayed holding a weapon, a dart or crossbow to start with, but then the scythe became the weapon of choice. Paintings of the time showed Death swinging his scythe in a fatal arc through a crowd of people, mowing down souls as if they were no more substantial than a field of wheat. The scythe was a symbol that resonated with the agricultural population of the time, where the autumn harvests represented the end, and by implication the death, of another year.

As Michael and I stood in our field and took turns at swinging our own scythe, these morbid thoughts were far from our minds. Instead we were concentrating on our swing, our posture, looking for the sweet spot and silently congratulating ourselves when we found it for a precious second before the next molehill destroyed the moment. Most of all we revelled in the peace and quiet, so different to the deafening whine of the strimmer. Now we heard nothing but the subtle swish-swish of the blade as it moved back and forth. In some symbolic way we felt that, where we had been fighting against nature with the strimmer and losing, now we were working with nature, quietly and gently, a far better solution for both of us.

Chapter 21

Off-grid house-sitting in the Spanish Pyrenees

❖ ❖ ❖

Within a few days we were on the move once more, heading just over the border into the Spanish Pyrenees. We had taken on a house-sit for a month over Christmas and the New Year in a remote, off-grid property with one dog, four cats and a pair of wild kites that the owners fed each day. It was situated at an altitude of around 850 metres along the Hecho valley north of Jaca and, at the moment, was below the snow line. Snow could arrive at this altitude any time from mid-December onwards, although some years it didn't arrive until January.

'So how do we feel about a white Christmas?' asked Michael.

'Yes and no,' I replied, gazing out of the window at the forest-clad slopes and thinking how beautiful they would look covered in snow. On the other hand, it would curtail our exploration of the area. The main roads would be kept clear, but it was the smaller roads that tempted us, tortuous and steep as they twisted and turned through gorges and high mountains.

'Ah, here it is.' I had been looking for the track from the valley road that would lead up to our new home. It was unmarked and led steeply up into the trees and then curved sharply out of sight. 'At least I hope this is it.'

As tracks go it was a decent track, but I could see immediately that there was no way we would get either up or down in icy or snowy weather. We had already been warned by the homeowners that if the weather was bad we would have to bring the van down the track and leave it close to the road if we wanted to get out. After a couple of hundred metres we came out of the trees and into a small clearing and there stood the house, made of stone, square and solid, built to withstand the weather. The setting reminded me of an amphitheatre, with the house centre stage, and the mountains rippling out in tiers from that centre. The lower levels, softly green with conifers, merged into the middle tier of rock and scree and then, right up in the gods, I could see the tip of snowy mountains. It had been raining earlier and now the mist was playing hide-and-seek in the trees around the house. There was a village about a mile away on the main road, but standing by the front door and turning 360 degrees all I could see was the mountains. It would be easy to believe we were the only people left in the world.

This house had been designed and built by its owners from scratch and was completely off-grid. On first impression, it was no different to a conventional house in terms of its amenities, with hot running water, fridge, freezer, washing machine, inside flushing loos and underfloor heating, but we were looking forward to seeing how they had constructed the off-grid systems which provided that power. I hate to admit it but I was perhaps a little less interested in how it all worked and more interested in simply enjoying hot running water and the rare luxury of a bath. If we want hot water at Le Shack we have to heat it up on the hob or the fire; on-demand, hot water straight from the tap is one of the hardest things to do without, particularly in a cold winter.

It soon became apparent that it was all a question of scale and if you have enough batteries and solar panels there are no limits. The storage capacity of batteries is measured in amp hours: our batteries stored 250 amp hours and serviced our tiny one- room cabin but we estimated that it would require around 1,500 amp hours to power a three-bedroom house. The inverter, a device which converts the power stored in the battery to power that can be used in a normal household 240-volt system, would need to be in the region of 5,000 watts whilst ours was 250 watts. A bank of solar panels were mounted on the outbuilding that housed the generator. A small wind turbine had been placed to catch the best of the wind and the entire system was automated, even to the point of a large diesel tank which automatically kept the generator topped up with fuel. This house was an excellent example of how much easier it is to construct an efficient off-grid system if the house is designed and built around it, rather than trying to retro-fit an established house that already has conventional lighting and heat sources. Of course, it isn't just about the practical elements of the system; it can't happen if the will is not there to do it in the first place. It seems a terrible shame to us that more houses aren't built like this.

The water supply to the house was provided from a network of open irrigation canals that ran the length of the valley with spurs coming down to farms and to residential homes and was collected in a 70,000-litre water tank. In summer, these canals can run dry and so water needs to be used sparingly. We walked up to see for ourselves where the water came from and found a concrete canal, completely open to the elements and about eighteen inches wide, with water running down it. To the left and right of it was a herd of cattle. When the owners had first moved here they had used this irrigation canal as a source of drinking water, but after a few experiences of feeling unwell now used it only for washing the dishes and showers. Drinking water was collected from springs in the mountains or down in the village in five-litre plastic bottles and these bottles needed to be regularly replenished.

'This is a first,' I said as I unloaded a batch of empty five-litre plastic water containers from the van.

We had parked up next to a narrow stone trough on a side street in the village. A continuous stream of water ran out of a pipe from one end and we used it to fill up our water containers, an experience that felt far more satisfying than just turning on the tap in the house, although I suspect some of that satisfaction was due to novelty value and it might not be such a good experience in a snowstorm or when the water had iced up. It felt as if I had been transported back into the past, and looking around the village square I almost expected to see donkeys and carts trundling through instead of cars.

❖❖❖

The dog was a large tan and white collie called Alfie, friendly and easy to live with. He had a great ruff of deep fur around his neck that reminded me of our old collie, Lucy, and he liked nothing more than to be given a good rub and a scratch around his neck in just the same way she did. He lived outside, by choice, but was allowed in the house whenever he wanted to be inside. He was nervous of thunderstorms and gunshot from the hunt and would whine to be let in if we didn't get to him first, but even on sub-zero, frosty nights he was happier outside, curled up in a basket of fleecy rugs.

The four cats were all rescue cats, each sleeping in different beds in the house, with different eating preferences and varying levels of paranoia, presumably as a result of their troubled backgrounds. Two were black, one a pretty tabby and the other looked as if someone had taken a selection of three different cats and grafted them together. Her body was completely white apart from one perfectly formed black dot on her side; her tail abruptly changed into black and tan stripes at the base where it joined her body and she had three black patches between her ears. Her eyes were red-rimmed and most of the time her pupils were the thinnest slit in the centre of her eye, giving her the appearance of being cross and slightly deranged. In fact she was the most affectionate of all the cats and loved nothing better than to crawl onto the nearest lap, preferably someone wearing black trousers, and shed a generous portion of her fur while she was there.

Occasionally there would be a spat as one cat ventured onto a sleeping spot that had already been claimed by another and, although nervous of us initially, they soon settled down. The same was true of ourselves, not with regard to arguments over who was to sleep where, but more to do with the process of settling in. It always takes a few days to feel comfortable with how a house runs, to find out where everything is rather than endlessly hunting through cupboards looking for a cheese grater, and to feel at ease, rather than being on best behaviour.

The kites were called Milana and Milano, a pair, who were

fed a couple of raw chicken wings or thighs at around 4pm each afternoon. *Milano* is the Spanish word for kite, and *milana* the female equivalent. They would arrive each day around lunchtime, circling high over the house and settling at the top of two trees on the right hand side of the field to keep an eye on who was about and when dinner would be served, a ritual which entailed cutting up the raw meat, throwing it out onto a patch of grass a reasonable distance from the house and then retreating indoors. A pair of crows would also turn up, taking their position in the trees on the left hand side. Then it was a waiting game.

We had been warned that the kites were very cautious and would only come down for the food when they thought no-one was about. All manner of things would be construed as a warning that it wasn't safe, such as a different car parked in the drive or even a shadow at the window, which was usually us, pressing ourselves against the side of the window in a bid to fool them that we weren't there. In years past we had visited a kite feeding station in Wales where any instinctive caution was thrown to the winds once the meat hit the ground and the birds, who were there in numbers, would swoop down regardless of how many onlookers peered out from the viewing huts or walked around the area. These mountain birds were less trusting. They had an ongoing feud with the crows, who also coveted this free handout. Milana and Milano, who had spent hours waiting for the meat to appear, would spend another hour checking that it was safe to come and get it but this caution was abandoned if a crow took a fly-by. Either one or both of them would suddenly snap to attention, lock onto their target and speed off to do battle, resulting in a tumbling free-for-all, the sleek midnight-black feathers of the crow offset against the rich red of the kite, until suddenly they would break away and resume their posts.

If we watched and waited for them to come down, nothing ever happened. If we got on with what we were doing and happened to look up at the right moment we might catch a flash of red from the corner of our eye as a bird dropped from the skies, twisting and diving with consummate skill and grace. It was one of those blink and you miss it wildlife experiences, but what is hard-won is always more rewarding.

Chapter 22

Sorry, I don't speak Spanish

❖ ❖ ❖

Every Thursday morning, around 11am, Oscar the Fishman drives his refrigerated truck and trailer up the winding, cobbled streets and parks in the village square of the tiny hilltop village of Embun in the Hecho valley. He opens up the sides of the trailer to reveal an instant vegetable and grocery shop: one side devoted to store-cupboard items and fruit, a sunny kaleidoscope of oranges and yellows, and the other to vegetables, the earthy tones of cabbages, spinach, carrots, potatoes, celery, aubergines, onions, garlic and leeks neatly arranged in tiers with handwritten scraps of paper telling you the price. His next job is to open the side of the refrigerated truck, and there is the fish counter, an exotic display of fish all freshly brought from the coast in the early hours of the morning. Within a few minutes of arriving he is open and ready for business. The nearest major supermarket from where we were staying is an eighty-kilometre round trip. Given the price of fuel these days and the fact that not everybody in these remote mountains has a car, Oscar and his van are an important part of village life.

Everybody knows what time he will arrive and on what day, and as we stood in the queue waiting our turn, I noticed people coming out of their houses, both men and women, shopping bags and purses in hand, many of them in slippers and baggy cardigans. When your shop is right outside your front door, there is no need to think too hard about what to wear. It soon became obvious that everybody knew each other, and that this weekly ritual was about more than just buying food. The conversation flowed and ebbed around Oscar, who kept up a constant dialogue with his audience, joking, laughing, gently chiding when one of his regulars accused him of not having one of her staples. He told her it was where it always was, she disagreed, and several of the other ladies marched her off and showed her that it was exactly where it should be. We didn't understand a single word that was spoken but sometimes life is like a pantomime and words are unnecessary.

There was a procedure to be followed. First of all people filled up their bags with the fruit, vegetables and other groceries from the trailer. The bag was then placed on a nearby bench and the order of the bags denoted the order of the queue. A customer may leave their bag temporarily, perhaps to chat to a neighbour or to go round the other side of the van as they had forgotten something, but that didn't mean some foreign interloper who had no idea of the natural order of things could contemplate stealing their place. The bag was then taken round to the side door, passed up to Oscar, who weighed it all, talking non-stop as he did so, and then the serious shopping began – the choosing of the fish.

From our experience that day it seemed that the Spanish were big fish-eaters. They knew what they wanted and took their time looking at what was on offer, asking Oscar to turn the fish over so they could check on the quality, to bring out another one that was bigger, or smaller or perhaps something different altogether. This was slow shopping and as long as you were not in a hurry it seemed to be a far more enjoyable experience than pushing a trolley through the aisles of a supermarket.

'That old lady has just spent over 100 euros,' I whispered to Michael.

'How do you know that?'

'I can see from the till display. And the one before her was even more than that.'

Watching what other people buy and how much they spend was a newly acquired habit of mine. I'm not sure what it says about me but once you start doing it, it becomes addictive. It started when we moved to France and our own shopping habits changed. We still went to the supermarket but it is a rare person who can move to a country like France and not use the local *boulangerie* or *boucherie* in the same way that the local people do. It never ceases to amaze me how much of the weekly budget is spent on bread, cakes and pastries as well as on meat and fish. From what we saw in the village square that day, people in Spain have the same ethos as the French.

Good food is worth a good price, one that respects the farmers and the fishermen as well as Oscar, who worked incredibly long days to ensure that his business remained viable. Having said that, a conversation with some English people who had lived in the village for over thirty years highlighted the fact that his prices had gone up substantially over the last year, understandable given the general economic situation, but there has to come a point when people start cutting back. Another factor that will have a long-term effect on the other small local shops, as well as Oscar and his mobile van, is the shrinking populations in these villages. Seventy-five years ago Embun used to be home to 800 people; now there are only sixty people living there all year round, and they are an ageing population. There is very little work here and so the young people do not stay.

At last it was our turn. Oscar beamed at us, started weighing our vegetables and chatted away. We had no idea what he was saying, couldn't even begin to guess at the odd word that sounded similar enough for us to put it in context. Michael has one sentence of Spanish to deal with this situation.

'*Lo siento, no hablo español.*'

Undeterred at our embarrassing inability to speak Spanish, Oscar switched to French. That was more like it! Now we were on familiar territory, but I was surprised. Perhaps he had seen our French number plates as we drove up and initially assumed we were French, but he must have heard us talking in English together as we waited in the queue. There is an assumption that most Spanish people will speak English, which may well be true in the tourist towns and well-known attractions, or in areas where there is a large community of expats, but there were relatively few English people in these valleys and the local people knew about as much English as we did Spanish.

There is a train of thought that suggests that being unable to speak the language of a country you are travelling through need not be a barrier, that it can add to the mystery and romance of the experience. As one human being to another we will always find a way to make ourselves understood, even if it comes down to hand signals and pointing at things. As they used to say in the good old bad old days, just raise your voice and shout! I can see that there is an element of truth in this, although not the shouting bit, but I think if the objective is to get to know a country and her people, this inability to communicate on any meaningful level must end up being a barrier. On a purely practical note, it can only make it harder to arrange the simplest of things. But equally importantly, talking to people and finding out about their lives is one of the great gifts of travelling and it would seem a waste of precious time not to be able to enjoy it as much as possible. Any relationship, even a fleeting one, is a two-way affair, and if a foreign visitor makes no effort to speak even a few words of the language, the relationship becomes all take and no give which doesn't work for anyone.

As the villagers smiled and tried to engage me in a conversation that I could not be part of, I realised that I should have made an effort to learn at least a few basic sentences. It was easy to make excuses: we were only here for a month, and we were living in such an isolated spot that the only other people we had seen were at the supermarket and at this mobile fish shop but, if nothing else, this taught me a valuable lesson for the future. I had become very comfortable in France, my language skills good enough for me to engage with people, although I was aware that I was coasting and a renewed effort was needed to reach the next level. As I stood in that market square in Spain, relying on an excessive amount of smiling and nodding of my head in a bid not to seem aloof or unfriendly, I could see so clearly how my lack of language skills was setting me apart. It was a shock, and a necessary wake-up call. We had plans to extend our travel further into Europe over the coming year and I made a mental note to myself that a phrase book would be on the list of 'must-have' travel items.

On a lighter note, here is an old French joke about a travelling salesman, not quite the same as a mobile shop but close enough to be relevant. The French word for a joke is *plaisanterie*, which sounds somehow more appealing but perhaps I am biased. This amusing French anecdote was translated and passed on to me by a fellow author and blogger, Vanessa Couchman, who writes about French life at www.lifeonlalune.com.

A travelling vacuum cleaner salesman arrives in a remote Cantal village and goes to a small house on the outskirts where an elderly lady lives. Before she can say anything he starts his sales spiel.

'Madame, *I'm going to demonstrate an absolute marvel, the new Cyclone vacuum cleaner. It sucks up everything in a few seconds. Where is your waste bin? In the kitchen? Allow me to fetch it.'*

He brings the waste bin into the sitting room and empties the contents onto the floor.

'Don't worry,' he says. 'With the Cyclone vacuum cleaner, I'll make all this rubbish disappear, down to the last crumb. Furthermore, if anything is left, I promise to eat it.'

'Just a minute, Monsieur. *I'd better bring you some salt and pepper,' said the old lady. 'I don't have electricity here.'*

Chapter 23

Christmas Day – home alone

❖ ❖ ❖

Christmas Day is traditionally a day for eating, drinking and being with family. Whilst our family back in the UK tucked into a huge meal, wearing paper hats, pulling crackers and wincing over the jokes, we were sitting on top of a hill eating cheese sarnies and home-made mince pies. We were supposed to have a cup of tea with it but somehow the mugs got left behind.

It might seem that this is a lonely way to spend Christmas Day – or perhaps it sounds heavenly and you are tempted to try it next year. Whatever life one leads, whether it be nomadic or static, no-one can be in two places at one time. When we first moved away from the UK and began travelling, there were times of the year when we missed family and friends more intensely, obvious examples being Christmas Day, New Year and birthdays. I can remember our first Christmas in France on *Olivia Rose* quite clearly. It was 2017, and we had decorated the boat, opened our Christmas presents, been out for a long walk with the dogs and all got soaked. We had planned a special evening meal but at one point it all felt flat, an anti-climax, as if some vital element was missing, which of course it was. By the time we'd had a couple of glasses of Prosecco balance was, thankfully, restored.

Since then we've learnt to adapt to our situation, doing something to mark these particular days in a pleasing way and accepting that our special times with family and friends will not be governed by fixed days of the year but will happen when we are actually with them.

And so on Christmas Day of 2022 we sat on a hilltop in northern Spain and looked down on the Yesa Reservoir, also known as the Pyrenean Sea, about an hour away from our house-sit. Behind us was a village called Tiermas, the walls a light sand colour, mellow in the unseasonably warm sunshine. This ancient settlement was situated on top of a hill, a perfect position for defence as it commanded a clear view in all directions. The valley had been flooded in the 1960s to make way for the reservoir, totalling a considerable catchment area of 2,089 hectares, constructed to provide a water supply for Zaragoza and a further thirty-five municipalities. This was a dry area of Spain and whilst the irrigation that came from the project benefited some communities, it destroyed others, notably the three villages of Tiermas, Esco and Ruesta. These few houses behind us were all that remained of Tiermas but nobody lived there any more, their livelihoods taken from them as the fields that they farmed disappeared under water. The houses on this hill were safe from the water itself, but the buildings became unstable as the land shifted, with landslides and cracks in the roads making them uninhabitable.

We picked our way over the rubble, past buildings with no roofs and gaping windows. Peering into small terraced cottages, where families would have shared their own Christmas meal years ago, we saw piles of stone and roof timbers sticking up at odd angles, abandoned where they fell. Spindly saplings had self-set in this barren ground and were growing up and out through the holes in the roofs whilst the brambles smothered everything, as they always do. The church would once have been the heart of the village but was now a sad place, graffiti scrawled over its crumbling walls, most of the roof gone, and the painted ceiling above the altar fading with each passing year.

Further down the valley was Esco, another ghost village, abandoned but for one man who stubbornly remained, looking after the animals on an adjoining farm. In total 1,500 people were displaced in this area and resettled, sometimes in completely new villages. There seems to be little record of how this resettlement worked in reality, and it is hard to know whether the local people put up a fight or were adequately compensated for their loss. In the present day, there are plans to dramatically increase the size of the reservoir further still and this is being fought by the local communities.

Standing amongst the tumble-down ruins, rubble all around us, it seemed such a terrible waste, more reminiscent of a war zone than the natural degradation that comes when humans move away and nature takes over. Given that Esco officially dates back to the twelfth century, the historical roots here would have been strong, with generations of families passing through these simple homes. It must have been very hard to leave.

Looking down to the flooded valley floor we could see the remnants of the thermal baths, part of the lower village of Tiermas, and could just make out ten or fifteen people floating in the warm, health-giving waters. As we walked down towards them we could smell the sulphur in the air and, dabbling our fingers in the turquoise waters, found it was indeed like a warm bath. Like everything else here the baths were a shadow of their former selves and in danger of total collapse, and if we hadn't seen with our own eyes that people still came here to bathe and to take advantage of the mud, allegedly good for the skin, it would have been hard to believe that anyone would choose to spend a few hours relaxing beneath dilapidated stone ruins.

These baths usually disappear beneath the water as the levels rise, but as of September this year the reservoir was at only 16% of its capacity and so the baths are still in use. Startling satellite pictures taken by Copernicus, the European Union's Earth Conservation Programme, show how the water level had sunk over the last three months as Spain suffered, like so many others, from a prolonged drought and confirmed what we could see with our own eyes. The weather patterns were changing and water was becoming a scarce commodity.

Later that evening we sat down to our Christmas meal and an excellent Spanish Rioja. It had been a good day, an unusual day where we had seen something different. A travelling life may take you away from your family, but it compensates in other ways. This had been a day when history and geography had come to life, transformed into an experience that would stay in our minds, filed away under the section marked 'Christmas Days'.

We were approaching New Year's Eve and the beginning of another year. Where do these years go to? They fly by ever faster. I would love to say that we will be having a wild party and dancing the night away, but as you have no doubt guessed by now, that is unlikely to happen. At least we have each other and that is good enough – plus a dog and four cats of course.

Chapter 24

Carrion eaters

❖ ❖ ❖

'It seems a weird thing to market as a tourist attraction,' I said as we followed the winding road deeper up into the mountains.

'What's weird about bird-watching?' asked Michael.

'Vultures are hardly in the same category as a robin or a blackbird. And we're not here to listen to the birdsong, we're here to watch them feed. On a dead cow, or a dead sheep. Pulling all the innards out and getting covered in blood and gore.'

'It's what vultures do. And a blackbird eats worms. It's all a matter of scale.'

'Not exactly. What vultures do naturally is to spot a dead carcass on the side of the mountain and go down and clear it up. I don't have a problem with that. It's a natural process. What happens here is a big truck arrives, full of dead cattle and sheep and goodness knows what else, upends them on some sort of feeding platform and then it's a free-for-all. There's nothing natural about that. Dinner served on a plate. We're domesticating the wildest of birds and it feels wrong, not to mention excessively grisly.'

'We don't have to go if you don't want to,' said Michael.

'Part of me wants to, and part of me doesn't. We're nearly there now. I can't see any birds wheeling about overhead so maybe the truck isn't coming today.'

We pulled off the road. There were no signs to confirm that this was the spot, or the place to park, but Michael had been for a walk not far from here in the previous week and seen the viewing hut from a distance. A gravel track curved around the contour of the hill and so we locked the van and followed it on foot.

'Still no sign of any birds,' said Michael, squinting up at the sky. 'Looks like we shan't see anything today.'

After walking along the track for 500 metres we saw a pair of metal gates and behind them a fenced-off area. On the other side of the gates was a large, shallow trough filled with a green-tinged liquid, presumably a disinfectant tray for the truck. The ground fell steeply away in front of it and then levelled out onto a small stony plateau, which was where the truck would deposit its load, tipping the animals out so they could roll down the slope and end up on the flat area. Something caught my eye on the ground in front of the gates, and as we came closer I could see that it was a ribcage, a spine and part of a skull. The rump of the skeleton was partially covered in fur, thick and coarse like that of a wild boar, although I hadn't heard of wild boar being disposed of in this way. Peering round the side of the fencing we could see the feeding area more clearly. The ground was covered in bones, all shapes and sizes, lying criss-crossed, entangled and mixed up so that it was impossible from this distance to work out what animal they had originally come from. There were an awful lot of them.

'You'd think there would be a smell,' said Michael. 'But there's nothing.'

Now he mentioned it I could see what he meant. Having spent so many years walking round the Welsh hills we knew what death smelt like. The rotting carcasses of dead sheep were not exactly a common sight, but they were a part of the landscape, and the foxes and badgers cleaned them up in the same way that the vultures did here. Given the sheer number of bones piled up on the grass below us, the smell could have been awful, but they were picked meticulously clean, no flesh, no skin, no fleece or cowhide. Just bones.

The track carried on past the gates for another 200 metres to the hut, a small wooden cabin with slotted openings in the front from which to watch the birds, but there seemed little point going to look at it today.

'Do we want to try again next week?' asked Michael, sounding subdued.

'I don't know. Let's get out of here. It's giving me the creeps.'

We walked back towards the car and I was struck by the silence. We were in a remote part of the mountains, with hardly any cars on the roads and no sign of any walkers, not unusual in this part of Spain. It was one of the world's quiet places and usually I love the silence that comes from being far away from other human beings but something about this emptiness felt sinister, gave me a tingle up my spine, a sense of being watched despite the fact that we were quite alone. I was glad when we reached the car and drove away.

We didn't see any vultures that day, but we saw them on many other occasions as we drove up narrow gorges and walked beneath sheer cliff faces, circling effortlessly in the sky high above us or sitting on craggy rocks, warming themselves in the sunshine. Although there are several different species of vulture that breed in this region, it is the griffon vulture that is the most regularly seen. One of the largest flying birds on earth, it has a wing span of up to 2.6 metres and incredibly powerful eyesight, able to spot a carcass from several kilometres away. They are scavengers, with a strong hooked beak for ripping and pulling a carcass apart, but their talons are weak, not designed to cause injury or death and so they are not killers, although there are reports of them taking young, sickly calves or lambs when food becomes scarce. Their digestive systems are extremely acidic allowing them to eat rotten meat without any ill effects.

The other vulture that might be seen, although less commonly, is the bearded vulture, slightly larger than the griffon. It feeds on bone marrow and has earnt the nickname of 'the bone-breaker' due to the habit of flying up high with the bone in its talons, and then dropping it onto rocks where it shatters, giving the bird easier access to the marrow. We found a bone lying on the rough ground immediately in front of the house during our stay here. It was big enough that it could only have come from the leg of a cow or perhaps a wild boar. I had a hankering to see a bearded vulture, not just because they are rare but also because it seemed more of a colourful bird, quite handsome in its way, but even though I scoured the skies each day after spotting the bone, the bone-breaker remained as elusive as ever.

For centuries vultures have survived by feeding on fallen carcasses on the hills but their numbers fell due to being hunted, by feeding on poisoned bait set for bears and wolves, and due to the changing face of the farming landscape. Their relationship with humanity has been an off-on affair and we are not the most reliable of partners. At times we have hunted them and poisoned them, at other times we have used them to clear up around slaughterhouses and as a cheap way of getting rid of animal by-products that we have no use for. Driven close to extinction, they came to rely on us for a food source that would allow them to breed and to flourish but this of itself has caused problems.

During the BSE crisis an EC ruling decreed that dead animals must be burned due to the risks of contamination, effectively cutting off the food source from feeding stations, and forcing the birds to leave their mountain eyries and hunt further afield. There were reports of large flocks flying long distances in search of food, and of live animals being taken in greater numbers. As a result farmers on both sides of the Pyrenees asked for permission to shoot them, despite the fact that these are protected birds. Things took a grim turn for the worse in May 2013 when a tourist slipped to her death in the French Pyrenees and was reportedly eaten by vultures before rescuers could reach her.

An article in the *Daily Mail* covered the story, explaining that the woman had slipped and fallen 1,000 feet down a slope on the Pic de Pista on the French side of the Pyrenees. It was assumed that she had died from her fall, but by the time the rescue team arrived all that was left was a pile of bones, her shoes and clothes. They estimated it took the griffon vultures forty to fifty minutes to eat the body. The rescue helicopter had seen large numbers of vultures circling in the vicinity but had not realised what had happened until they found the remains.

The day after I read this article I counted thirty-five vultures circling directly above the house. Some were so high that I almost fell over backwards trying to see them, but others were much closer, close enough to make out the details on their wings. Something must have died in the area. On another occasion we spotted ten or fifteen birds perched on a rocky outcrop as we walked Alfie the dog along the river on his morning walk. They flew off as we drew nearer, always keeping their distance, vigilant and wary, fearing us more than we might be nervous of them.

The first impression of these birds is that they are incredibly ugly, but when you start to look more closely, the ugliness fades and they become fascinating. I can only admire how evolution has produced a creature so perfectly equipped for the job that it does, but am also saddened that they have to rely on us for their survival, especially now that the pastoral landscape is under threat, with farmers having children who want a different life. The feeding stations have returned since the BSE crisis, presumably under strict controls, but there is a delicate balance between supporting a species and over-feeding it, which causes a chain reaction that benefits neither us nor the birds.

We never did go back to the feeding station. It was enough to watch them wheeling above the mountains, powerful wings carrying them effortlessly up on the thermals. A magnificent sight.

Chapter 25

Walking with Alfie

❖ ❖ ❖

It was early January 2023 and snow was in short supply in the Spanish Pyrenees. From the windows of our house-sit I could see a light dusting of snow on the highest peaks. When we arrived in mid-December it had been a solid covering, blindingly white in the sun, but each day it had melted a little more and now the rock below was showing through. On the lower slopes it had melted days ago.

The newspapers were full of reports of ski resorts throughout Europe closing due to warmer than average temperatures. Others were relying on artificial snow, although that also was in short supply due to the ongoing water shortage, and others had opened up their summer biking and hiking trails as an alternative sport in an effort not to lose their winter tourist business.

During our stay there we came to know two close friends of the people that we were house-sitting for, an English couple who had lived here for thirty years. Niki teaches English and Richard is a walking guide and ski instructor. Both of them know the region very well and have first-hand experience of how dramatic changes in the weather can make it difficult to earn a living.

'The ski season usually opens in the first week of December and runs until Easter,' Niki told us. 'But it hasn't happened this year. The only way they can keep the downhill ski slopes going is by using artificial snow as a short-term measure and hope the real thing arrives soon.'

'I do quite a bit of cross-country ski-guiding,' added Richard. 'But with no snow on the lower levels I've had no work so far this winter. I'm also one of thirty instructors at a centre where we teach the school groups. We need snow in the next few days or they'll start to cancel their bookings.'

'We've all been talking about the effects of climate change for twenty years or more,' said Niki. 'But there's no doubt it's getting worse.'

Both of them were philosophical about their way of life being governed by the weather. There were good years and bad years and they had no choice but to take the rough with the smooth, but I could sense a new low had been reached this year.

'This winter is a tragic milestone,' said Richard. 'Who knows where we go from here?'

Despite all the long-term signs that the ski season is getting shorter and will continue to do so, the regional government of Aragon is ploughing huge amounts of money into new ski runs. It suggests that they are in denial about what is happening in front of their eyes and seems a terrible waste of funds, especially when that money could be used to build new opportunities that work with the changing climate, rather than doggedly holding on to something that is no longer sustainable.

We may have been lacking in snow, but the weather turned cold in that final week and treated us to some exquisite hoar frosts. Michael, Alfie and I set off for the usual morning walk, crunching our way across the flat ground in front of the house. A narrow track wound from the edge of the field across the contour of the hill although, as with many of the tracks in these mountains, it was so well camouflaged by conifers, box and a low-growing prickly scrub that caught at our knees as we picked our way over the rocky surface that you would never have known it was there. Alfie went ahead of us, perky despite suffering from arthritis, delighted as always to be out but coming back regularly to see why we weren't keeping up. He was one of those dogs who made you feel that he was taking you out for a walk, rather than the other way round. Arriving at a junction we parted ways, Michael heading off on a longer walk and Alfie and I taking the easier option and following a track along the river.

There is something special about a hoar frost. It transforms the most ordinary of things into tiny nuggets of absolute beauty if one walks slowly and takes the time to look for them. I stopped to admire the moss on a stone wall, frozen solid, the ice crystals sparkling like tiny diamonds. The branches of a plantation of young birches had been immortalised in white brush strokes, a frozen, petrified forest growing in the boulders beside the almost-dry river bed. I stopped so often to exclaim in delight at some tiny miracle that Alfie became restless, whining with a gentle impatience ahead of me. If I ignored him he would come closer and stick his snout pointedly into the back of my knees.

All dogs are not created equal. We have had three dogs of our own and looked after a fair number of other people's dogs through our house-sitting. They all have distinct characters and some are easier to be with than others. Alfie was a rare creature, the best of dogs. He had a natural dignity, a considered way of looking at his world, and the ability to communicate an astonishing number of things just by the way he tilted his head and looked at you with those big eyes. We hadn't been with him for long, just some more humans passing through his life, but we had become very attached to him. He was everything that you could ask for from man's best friend.

Eventually I decided it was time to turn back. He was beginning to limp a little, a sure sign that he was beginning to feel his arthritis, but I soon realised that he wasn't following me. I retraced my steps and found him round the next corner, waiting in the middle of the track. He turned and looked onwards, then back at me, his message clear. This is the thing with animals; they operate under different rules than we do. If he was aware of discomfort in his joints, it wasn't something he was going to take any notice of, or at least not at this stage, and as far as he was concerned this walk was not over. Unfortunately for him, we had been asked to limit his walking to a certain amount of time and we had reached it. A golden rule of house-sitting is to respect the owners' wishes with regard to their animals. I called him to me and turned back towards home. Having made his point, he followed me.

In a few days we would be leaving. If animals play by their own rules so also does time, sometimes going slowly, other times racing past and making a nonsense of human efforts to constrain it by the arbitrary measurement of hours and minutes, days and weeks. We had been here for almost a month and it felt both less and more than that. I took a long look at the mountains around me, committing their shapes and colours to memory.

I recently had a clear-out of photos from my camera, freeing up space for the coming year. I can't do the same thing for my personal memories, although I am sure my mind does it without me knowing, randomly deleting the pictures that I hold in my head, erasing the emotions that went with them, uncaring of how precious they might have been. Without my personal diaries, the blog and books that I write, it would be impossible to remember all the places we have visited, even harder to reconnect with how we felt, our highs and our lows. Does it matter if those memories fade, pushed aside by the urge to take new pictures and to write fresh words? Is there an art to maintaining our connection with our past, which in so many ways defines who we are, without dwelling on it at the expense of who we will be in the future?

Ahead of me Alfie trotted down the stony track, pausing every now and then to sniff at something that caught his attention, and I smiled at the simplicity of his life. Not all questions need an answer and this was a moment for walking, not thinking.

Chapter 26

Beware the boulangerie

❖ ❖ ❖

'I'm just popping out to get some bread,' I called to Michael as I hopped onto my bike.

'Popping out' didn't quite give an accurate description as the nearest *boulangerie* from Le Shack was a fifteen-mile round trip. We could buy bread from a house in the nearest village, but they were open at limited times and only sold white baguettes. We didn't eat white bread, fussy I know, and the *boulangerie* in Lembaye made lovely bread, granary and dark rye, and many other things besides.

Michael appeared from the depths of the shed, scythe in hand. We were newly returned from the Spanish Pyrenees and after a month away, there was gardening work to be done.

'Remember...' He paused and I finished the sentence off for him.

'I know, I know. *Beware the boulangerie.*'

This had become our mantra for buying bread. The thought behind it was that if whoever was buying the bread repeated it to themselves enough times as they crossed the street and pushed open the door to the shop it would arm them with sufficient strength of mind to come away with just bread, and not be seduced into buying other goodies that were bad for both the waistline and the budget.

An *artisan* granary loaf would set you back between two to four euros depending on where you bought it from and it might last two days, although that wasn't a given if Michael was feeling particularly hungry. In his defence these are not big loaves, roughly a third of the size of a packet of the sliced tasteless stuff from a supermarket. We never have our bread sliced as we like to cut it ourselves, thick-cut bordering on doorstop measurements, and it tastes so good that we don't resent a penny of it. However, a minimum of three loaves a week adds up to an average figure of thirty-six euros a month spent on bread. The problem comes when you add in a chocolate and hazelnut brownie to enjoy with a morning coffee, and a savoury quiche for lunch, and then there are the sweet tarts – raspberries and strawberries, apricots and pears, almonds and apples, a mouth-watering choice of fruits delicately arranged in perfect circles on a pastry base. This is where it gets expensive and before you know it, you've spent ten or fifteen euros. We could spend forty-five euros in this *boulangerie* every week without thinking twice, which comes in at a sobering 180 euros a month for bread and cakes. Hence our new slogan '*Beware the boulangerie*'.

Full of good resolutions, I set off on my bike. I could have taken the van, but we had left our bikes behind whilst in the Spanish Pyrenees, reasoning that the mountain gradients would be a step too far for our sort of cycling, and I was desperate to feel the fresh air rushing past my cheeks in the way that only happens when you are on a bike. Before opening the gate I tentatively checked to see that the neighbour's dog wasn't outside on the road. Her name is Immanole, and she's a Pyrenean guarding dog with tendencies towards paranoia and schizophrenia. If we see her with her owner, she's the sweetest thing, coming up to nuzzle your hand and give it an ingratiating lick. If she's by herself, she undergoes a Jekyll-and-Hyde transformation and decides we are the least favourite thing in her world. She barks and runs at us aggressively, baring her teeth and, whilst she hasn't taken a chunk out of us yet, it's only a matter of time. She also loves chasing bikes. Thankfully the road was clear.

We live in a series of undulating valleys, very different from the terrain that we had just left, but still with enough ups and downs to give my legs and lungs a good workout. The first bit is always easy, downhill past the organic vegetable farm, over the river and then the climb begins. Gently at first, past the free-range chicken farm, a very recent business venture, now sadly no longer a going concern. We had watched with approval and anticipation as the young man who had bought this small patch of land and the ruin of a cottage that went with it fenced off an enclosure and built his own sheds, not much bigger than those that we had on our own smallholding years ago. Before long he had a collection of ducks, geese and chickens, all looking healthy and happy. The last time we called in to pick up a dozen eggs he told us he was no longer selling to the public. The cost of grain had become prohibitive, and his customers couldn't afford the price he would have to charge to cover his costs. Although he didn't mention it I suspect the bird flu situation was also a contributing factor. Most of the chickens are gone now, sold on to other people, and he has kept just a few to provide eggs for his own consumption. All we can do is hope that things get better and he can open up again at some point in the future.

From here it is a long, slow pull up the hill, but the route is so beautiful that it is always worth the effort. The single-track road snakes its way up to the ridge line through woodland, bronze beech leaves carpeting the ground, dappled in the winter sunshine. I use this hill to measure my fitness levels. If I reach the top in *tour* mode I am pleased with myself. If I weaken and click up to *sport* then I know it's time to try harder. Using *turbo* is just pathetic. Coming out of the woods at the top of the hill in *tour* mode, I give myself a congratulatory pat on the back, and turn onto a larger road. From here a series of gentle undulations leads through fields that in summer will be golden with sunflowers and maize. For now they are either stubble or bare earth, a harvest in waiting. As usual there is hardly any traffic, only two passing cars all the way into town, and I can imagine that the entire sweeping vista is mine and mine alone.

I had enjoyed our time in both the Alps and the Pyrenees, but this less austere landscape is where I feel more at home. The high mountains were unquestionably magnificent but there was always the sense that they could crush you so easily, that a slight shift in the weather would turn them against you. I felt as if I was constantly looking over my shoulder, wary of the clouds coming down in a heartbeat, of my world shrinking, of being lost in the mist. Nature had two faces in this grand landscape, one benign and the other hostile and, over the winter months in particular, it was hard to predict when the mood would change. The walking was also very different, the tracks so steep and stony that I hardly dared to take my eyes off them, placing each footstep with care. In the less well-trodden valleys the paths would sometimes disappear altogether. So much of the landscape was unreachable, sheer rock faces or impenetrable forests, a look-but-don't-touch panorama. In contrast, I can go anywhere I please in the landscape around Le Shack, whatever the weather. It offers an endless playground of walking trails through forests and by rivers, and a maze of country lanes, perfect for cycling, that offer glimpses of reservoirs through the trees or lead me through the quiet streets of picturesque villages.

I cycled the last kilometre through the backstreets of the town and parked the bike in the main square. There is often a queue for bread, with people waiting outside the door, but that morning the shop was empty. The previous evening I had read an article in *The Local*, an online magazine for expats, which highlighted the problems now facing thousands of French *boulangeries*. Production costs were out of control, eggs costing more because of bird flu, flour more expensive because of the war in Ukraine, with knock-on effects on the price of butter, almonds, sugar, paper and cardboard packaging for the cakes. Worst of all was the cost of energy which was threatening to send many of them out of business. According to Franceinfo, one of the mainstream French news channels, 80 per cent of them were at the risk of bankruptcy.

The *boulangerie* is the heart of any village or town, but its significance goes deeper than that. It is a symbol of what France is all about, an expression of its values and the belief that food is not just food but a way of sharing in each other's lives. These little shops, often family-run, have been struggling to survive in rural parts of France for years now, but it was unthinkable that they could disappear in such huge numbers. I could feel myself going into denial at the mere suggestion of it.

I walked up to the counter and asked for my bread. I put my hand in my purse but then I weakened. This little business needed to be supported by its customers and besides, we'd been away in Spain for a month where the bread shops had surprisingly little to tempt us with. As far as the bread mantra was concerned we must have been in credit so it was time to share the spoils.

'I'll have two of those please,' I said, pointing to the muffins. 'And perhaps a couple of tarts as well.'

I cycled back up the hill to Le Shack feeling that all was well in my world. I knew this was another illusion, that in fact I couldn't remember the beginning of a year with so much to worry about: extreme weather around the globe, the hospitals full of people with flu and Covid, the war in Ukraine, the cost of living crisis, people on strike for more money and better working conditions and an overwhelming sense of general discontent in the land. But that is the beauty of cycling through the hills on a sunny winter's morning. You can make everything else go away, for a little while at least.

Cycling up to our front gate, I tensed. Immanole had a habit of lying down next to one of the dilapidated vehicles that clog up our neighbour's parking area. It was difficult to know whether she was there until it was too late. I cycled quietly up the hill, breathing a sigh of relief as our gate came into view. I had made it. I swung off my bike, ready to open the gate and reach a safe haven, but then there she was, tottering on unsteady legs as she must have been asleep, lips curled back from snarling teeth, barking maniacally and eyeing up my ankles with malicious intent. I bundled myself and the bike through the gate and left her to it.

'That dog has hardly stopped barking since you left. She barks at me, at a car going past, at a tractor over the other side of the valley. She's much worse than she used to be and she's driving me absolutely nuts.' This was an unusually long tirade from Michael, who is adept at zoning out things he doesn't want to hear. 'I almost went round to see them about it, but I know it's pointless. I think she's lost the plot, got doggy dementia if there is such a thing. Another couple of weeks of this and I'll be the one with dementia.'

'You sound like you need a nice cup of tea,' I said soothingly.

'What I really need is a chocolate muffin.'

'Well, it's funny you should say that...'

'Ha! I knew you'd weaken. What else did you get?'

He rummaged around in the saddle bag.

'Raspberry tarts, fantastic. I'll get the kettle on.'

We left Immanole outside, still barking. Nothing in life is completely perfect.

Chapter 27

Musings from a settled life – but not for long

❖ ❖ ❖

In exactly the same way that it takes us a few days to settle into a new house-sit it also takes us a while to settle back into a non-travelling life. Sometimes we have been away from Le Shack for so long that it is no longer familiar and we have forgotten where things are, looking in the wrong place for a particular utensil or scratching our heads as to where we keep the kitchen towels. Then there are the practical matters, such as having no running hot water. We heat a pot on the woodburner for washing up, and for a shower we put two big pans on the gas hob which we tip into a bigger plastic bucket once they are hot. This system gives us a good shower, with plenty of hot water and pressure from a small pump at the bottom of the plastic bucket, but we have to think about it half an hour before we want one. And we wouldn't dream of having a shower in the morning when the fire has gone out and Le Shack is at its coldest. Showers are now a pre-dinner ritual in the evening when the cabin is warm and cosy.

The weather has turned properly wintry, which is a relief in a way as it is at least normal, but washing your hands in glacial water when it is below zero outside is not a pleasant experience. As for going to the loo, well, it's outside so that also cools us down! As I write this I can imagine that the reader is shuddering with horror at such a spartan existence, but I am continually surprised at how simple it is to ease our way back into it and how it sounds much worse than it is. The reason we spend so little time here is not because we struggle with a lack of hot water or miss a warm inside loo, but simply because we get itchy feet. We've lost the habit of staying in one place for long and get a little panicky if the diary stretches ahead with no trips pencilled in.

It's not surprising that we never really settle in the way that we used to when we had a normal house and lived there for most of the year, year in, year out. In that life, I had a structure that could only be built and maintained by physically being there: obviously there was work but I also went to yoga classes, writing classes, was a member of various local groups. Because we knew we would be there, we could book theatre tickets weeks in advance and arrange summer BBQs and winter walks with friends. All these things tether you to a place, grounding you in a good way, but we live in a foreign country where we began with a clean slate, knowing nobody and with a foreign language to navigate our way through. When you combine that with the fact that we are rarely at Le Shack for longer than a few weeks spread out over the year, it seems unlikely that we will ever begin to put down roots and yet we are, although they are more like delicate tendrils than substantial roots at this stage.

We have become friends with a like-minded English-speaking couple called Ev and Sue in the next village and it gives me a warm feeling to know that I can knock on their door in passing and be made welcome. This January, by pure chance, we were here for our own village's annual gathering to share the *galette des rois*, or the 'kings' cake', which historically marks the arrival of the three wise men, or kings, in Bethlehem to deliver gifts to the baby Jesus. Due to the pandemic it had not taken place over the last two years, so the relief that things were back to normal made it a special occasion. Everyone who lives in the village is invited, with cakes, cider and wine provided by the *mairie*. I never find it easy to walk into a room full of strangers but avoiding it would have seemed churlish and unfriendly, so we took a deep breath and plunged in.

'*Ah, vous êtes les anglais*' was the common response, followed by a handshake or *la bise*, the traditional greeting kiss, one on each cheek. During the pandemic this familiar French way of greeting had been replaced by less intimate ways of saying hello, but in our village hall on a cold Sunday in January *la bise* was acceptable once more and nobody was going to miss an opportunity to make up for all those lost kissing moments, even if it meant going cheek to cheek with a couple of foreigners.

People arrived in dribs and drabs, taking off their coats, rubbing their hands together and moaning about how cold it was. Apart from the kissing it could have been a village hall in the UK; almost all of them came up and greeted us as we nervously loitered on the edges, giving me a sudden flashback to the local disco in my teens where I had done an excellent impression of being a wallflower. They knew who we were and where we lived; they wanted to know if we liked it here and when we explained that we spent most of our time travelling, they nodded with approval and understanding. The men came up, patted Michael on the shoulder and told him jokes, proving that laughter or a smile goes a long way in making a connection. We were the only English people there, as expected, and whilst there was the odd, tortured attempt to speak a little English for our benefit, it didn't last long. We didn't expect it to. The onus was on us to speak their language and that was as it should be.

After about an hour and a half we made our excuses and left. It is surprisingly tiring trying to talk for that amount of time in a foreign language where you know enough to get by, but not enough to be able to keep up with everything that is said.

'That wasn't so bad after all,' said Michael as we walked to the car. 'A friendly bunch. Nice people.'

'Yes they were,' I agreed. 'Did you understand any of those jokes?'

'Not a single one. But I think I bluffed my way through. Perhaps I'll have to learn one to share with them for next year. But then we probably won't be here...'

❖ ❖ ❖

It's 9am and in the woods that surround our field a deer is making its way through the tangled undergrowth. Our trail camera is attached to a tree not far away, and the movement of the deer triggers it. There is an imaginary silent click and a picture is stored on the SD card. Each time the animal moves it activates the camera, and as we sit in the cabin a few days later looking at these images on our laptop, we can hardly make the deer out through the dense latticework of twigs and branches. It blends perfectly into the background, and all we can see is a hint of its head or body. But then it comes nearer and we realise that it has seen the camera. Warily it weaves its way closer, curious rather than scared, and now the camera is taking shot after shot. It is a male, the new season's growth of antlers sprouting from his head, soft and velvety.

Deer grow and shed their antlers each year. The new growth is covered with a hair-like membrane called 'velvet', a term which aptly describes it, but this is a vulnerable stage as cuts or bruises sustained now can result in deformed antlers later. The antlers grow and die in a cycle that ensures the deer will have a mature set of antlers for the breeding season. At the beginning of the cycle they are composed of a mixture of water and dry matter, with the water being the major component. The dry matter is made of protein, calcium and phosphorous. As the summer draws to an end growth slows and the antlers begin to harden. The velvet sloughs off, or is rubbed off, often within just twenty-four hours, resulting in hard, polished antlers. Now the deer is ready for the breeding season, equipped to fight other males. His antlers are also a sign that he is a male of quality, a visual testament to his strength and virility. After the breeding season the cells located at the point where the antlers are attached to the head begin to demineralise, weakening the connection and allowing the antlers to fall off. We have often looked for antlers in the woods and never found any. The reason is that the protein and calcium content is attractive to rodents, and they are usually devoured very quickly once they have fallen.[16]

Coming back to our own deer, he has taken a few more steps and is looking directly at the camera. There is a bare patch on his neck where he has rubbed at the fur, and we can see the detailed nuance of colour on his snout as he pushes it tentatively closer, so close that it almost touches the lens. There is a wide-eyed innocence about him as those big black eyes seem to gaze directly at us and then, slowly and calmly, he moves on, fading into the forest like some magical creature.

We rely on this trail camera to give us an insight into a hidden world, one we would never see otherwise. In the past we have seen a fox with its head held high, a dead chicken between its jaws, and a flash of a stone marten, there for a second and then

---

[16] Source: University of Missouri, https://extension.missouri.edu, 'Ecology and Management of White-tailed Deer in Missouri', Robert A. Pierce II, Jason Sumners and Emily Flinn

gone. We have seen a wild boar, or rather the rump of a wild boar as it jumped over a fallen tree and disappeared into the darkness. They live in groups, but we have only ever seen a lone animal. The camera has also picked up the hunting dogs, and even the hunters themselves, treading carefully, paying no heed to the fact that they were on private land. Many of the pictures were taken at night, or the early hours of the morning, using infrared, and it has been a reassuring barometer of the wildlife that still survives here.

A few months ago, on one of our previous visits to Le Shack, Michael walked up to check on the camera and found that the SD card was gone. This puzzled us, not just because of how it might have happened but as to who would have taken it. It could not have accidentally fallen out and it was on our land in a stretch of woodland with no footpaths. We later found out that the hunt also use trail cameras to monitor the movements of the animals, so perhaps they took it, mistaking it for one of their own cameras. We shall never know. We have purchased a new SD card and are locating it in a different area. For now, it remains intact.

❖❖❖

We have snow at Le Shack! Despite the fact that we can see the Pyrenees on a clear day, we are actually around sixty kilometres away and at a much lower altitude. It is unusual to see snow here and if it does come, it is a light dusting and doesn't last long. Even on a fleeting visit snow is a magical thing. It changes our world, bleaching it to a black and white landscape, turning trees into living sculptures and deadening sound until all is quiet. It turns us into children again, with thoughts of snowmen and toboggans and playing just for the sake of it. As I walk across our field all I can hear is the scrunch of my boots on the snow and the cawing of our resident pair of crows as they dive-bomb each other, hurtling towards the earth and then soaring up and the game begins again. Perhaps they too have been caught up in the joy of the moment.

More than any other weather phenomenon, snow is a memory-maker. I don't know why this should be so, but one possible explanation is that it is rare and it completely changes what we can see and what we can do. As a child I can remember going out with my mother to help my younger brother with his paper round in Suffolk. We'd had a massive amount of snow, far more than we seem to get these days, and the village roads were blocked. There was no way he could do it on his bike so the three of us did it on foot. In my mind I can clearly see us, a mother and her two children, hats and scarves bright against the whiteness, every step an adventure.

More recently I can remember a winter back in Wales on our smallholding when the temperature dropped to minus 10 and I had to break a thick sheet of ice on the water buckets for the animals every morning, sliding my way down the lane on a solid bed of snow that had iced over on top, every step a battle to stay upright. Another memory is of our cottage in Snowdonia, high on the hill, when the snow completely filled the single-track lane that was our only access. It was a sunken lane, bordered by high hedges, and the wind had blown the snow down into it and then swirled it around, like a food mixer running amok among egg whites, creating drifts five feet high. It took a tractor three days to open it up again and the neighbours further down the hill battled up through the fields, where the snow was only a few inches thick, turning up on our doorstep, faces ruddy in the cold air, bringing some fresh milk and vegetables.

Here at Le Shack our white world didn't last for long. Within 24 hours it had disappeared but in a way I was glad. There was no time for it to lose its pristine splendour, turning into a grey sludge by the side of the road, or for me to tire of it, irritated because I couldn't get out and about. The snow may have gone but the wintry theme stayed with us, several weeks of cold, frosty weather and sub-zero temperatures.

I have noticed since we've lost both our dogs that I don't walk as much as I used to, easily slipping into the bad habit of letting the weather dictate the level of activity, rather than giving in to a pair of beseeching eyes and a madly wagging tail persuading me to put on my walking boots and coat whatever the weather. On one of these frosty mornings I gave myself a good talking-to and ventured out alone, swaddled in layers of clothing and a thick scarf. As I set off across the track, shoulders hunched against the wind, I could hear the crump of frost beneath my feet. The pond was iced over, as were the drainage ditches that ran alongside the lanes. In one of the ditches, the ice had solidified in swirling patterns, like the age rings you see in a tree trunk or in planks of wood.

There was a crashing in the woods, twigs snapping, and I spotted a deer, running in mindless, panicky flight through the trees. It was a young one, alone, and paid me no heed, focused only on escape. I knew the hunt were out as I had heard the dogs barking while I finished my morning tea. A few moments later I flinched at the crack of a single gunshot. It was hard to know exactly where it came from as the sound reverberated around the hills but I guessed they were still some distance away. When we first moved here we had been nervous of gunshot, curtailing our walks, trying to second-guess where they might be. Of necessity we had become used to it, but it wasn't something we accepted easily and we weren't alone. From a poll conducted by IFOP in December 2022, almost 80 per cent of the French public favour a hunting ban on Sundays. It doesn't seem unreasonable to ask for one day of the week when people can walk in the countryside without fear of being shot. The hunting lobby is a powerful one but they are a minority. The government had an opportunity to do something about this under a recent review of the law but went for a less controversial option, offering tighter rules against hunting under the influence of drugs or alcohol and better training and safety systems, all of which rely on cooperation from the hunting groups and are difficult to enforce. *Plus ça change.* Nothing changes.

Eventually I turned off the lane and cut across what was usually a grassy field but was now newly ploughed. Unexpectedly a memory of our dog Maddie in this same field came into my mind, her soft spaniel ears flapping madly as she raced off into the distance. It caught me unawares, a sharp pang of loss. The water in the heavy soil had frozen solid, the clods of earth forming a brittle, unyielding terrain, where it would be so easy to twist an ankle, and each step sounded as if I was walking on broken glass. My only company was a buzzard, playing hide-and-seek in the high trees, there one moment and gone the next. Now I was only a few minutes from home, glancing up a track to see if the rabbits were still in their cages at a semi-derelict farmhouse. The building had such an air of neglect that the rabbits were the only obvious proof that anybody lived there at all. A hundred yards further on was another farmhouse, empty since we had been here, but this one had the potential to be a lovely home for someone. The owners were both dead and now it was mired in the depths of French inheritance tax laws. Turning up the hill towards Le Shack I could see the signs of wild boar rooting around in the verge on the side of the road. We had even seen one in our field on a recent afternoon, trotting purposefully from one corner to the other in broad daylight. I hadn't seen a soul on this walk, or at least not a human one, but this was not unusual. There are times in rural France when it can seem as if you are quite alone, the only person in the world – apart from the hunters, of course.

Walking back into the cabin after my walk, I found Michael peering at the laptop.

'What are you looking at?' I peered over his shoulder and smiled. 'I wondered how long it would take.'

'It can't do any harm to see if there's anything we might fancy,' he said, as he scrolled down through the latest house-sits available on the TrustedHousesitters website. 'There's a nice one down in the south, very close to the Mediterranean...'

It was late January and we had been back at Le Shack for two weeks. We had nothing in the diary between now and early April, which was when we headed back to *Olivia Rose*, and neither of us could imagine staying put for another two months in deepest winter. It had only ever been a matter of time before we started looking for something to fill the gap, and now it was time to get back out on the road.

Chapter 28

Why do we travel?

❖ ❖ ❖

When we sold our house and began this new life six years ago we had a plan. We had enough money to allow us to travel full time on our boat, *Olivia Rose*, for two years. After that we would need to do some sort of work on a part-time basis to earn enough to keep going with this lifestyle. Within three months of buying the boat those plans were derailed. The engine unexpectedly failed and the cost of buying and installing a new one took nearly all the funds we had put aside for those two years. Our solution was to limit our cruising to six months over the summer and go back to the UK to earn some money over the winter. We did this for two winters, but struggled to make what we needed.

Along came the pandemic and a succession of lockdowns and suddenly going back to the UK was no longer an option. At the same time, Brexit happened and we were forced to choose between the UK and France. We chose France, but had to buy a property so that we could stay here. This was yet another unexpected and unwanted assault on our dwindling savings, but help came from an unexpected quarter. I started writing a series of books about our life, and the income from those books was enough to allow us to continue to travel, albeit on a tight budget. Life throws both challenges and opportunities at all of us, and we adapt as best we can.

We have come to realise over the last six years that the freedom to travel is the one thing that matters to us above all else. Whether we travel by boat or bike, by camper van or by house-sitting, this lifestyle defines who we are and what we do.

Why do humans have such an irresistible urge to travel? We've done it since our earliest beginnings, marching across land in search of glory and wealth. Mountaineers risk their lives to reach the highest peaks and sailors cross oceans single-handed simply because they are there and demand to be conquered. In modern society our motivations are different, saving all our money so we can escape into a different reality. We might still look for a challenge, for a new experience, but we are also looking for respite from responsibility, a chance to slow down, to give our bodies and minds a break from the stress of working life.

Some people become famous because of their achievements, but ordinary people can also walk out of their front doors and begin the most amazing of adventures. As they walk a long-distance trail, or cycle through countries where the social norms are so different to their own, they are not just hungry for a new experience but are often looking for meaning, to make sense of something that has happened in their lives or to understand who they are. Every journey has two parts, one physical and one emotional, each as important as the other.

We travel because we are running away from something or towards something, because we need to know what's around the corner, because we need something to look forward to apart from the daily grind of the nine to five. We travel to be inspired, to be challenged, to follow a dream or to find out who we really are and what we want from our lives. How wonderful that one word can mean so many things to so many different people.

It's impossible to ask why humans as a whole are so fascinated by travel and then not ask myself the same question. Why do I do it? If I had to condense it into one sentence I would say that when I am travelling I feel truly alive, but the real answer is more complex than just those few words. I am evidently a restless spirit, greedy for life, and I don't seem to have what it takes to settle, to put down roots, to embrace a routine and a sense of security. I'm not aware of any major personal demons that I am running from, apart from myself at times, but no matter where

I go my self comes with me so there is no escape.

The very thought of what lies round the next bend is exciting; the challenge of pushing myself both scares and exhilarates me, and the chance to understand other cultures makes my world a richer place. It's like going to a school where the lessons are never boring, although at times they may be hard. I can see with my own eyes how the world is changing, talk to people in different walks of life and understand how these changes can affect them personally. History, economics and geography all come alive and mean something more than a mind-numbing stream of statistics. The constant traveller learns and grows as part of the journey, and whilst on the outside they may seem the same person, something changes inside.

We can't know with absolute certainty that our plans and dreams will happen as we expect them to and the discipline of being open to change and able to adapt to unforeseen events is one of the greatest lessons that I have learnt over the past six years. Since the pandemic, I have a different view of the way things work, understanding how quickly everything that we take for granted can be turned upside down. However the pandemic is only a part of it, one factor among many which can push us off the path we wanted to take: climate change and weather patterns, politics and wars, social unrest and future, unknowable health issues all have a part to play. I might be a hopeless romantic and a dreamer at heart, but this travelling life has taught me the value and necessity of being a realist as well.

Chapter 29

What next?

❖ ❖ ❖

It's early March 2023 and I am sitting on a beach looking out at the Mediterranean in the south of France. The air temperature is 20 degrees, and I have rolled up my trousers and stuck my feet into the sand. I close my eyes and feel the sun on my face.

We have been here for a month, staying in a town house in the pretty artist's village of Pézenas, a twenty-minute drive from the coast, looking after two dogs and a cat, but our time here is coming to an end. All around me the promise of spring is in the air: apple and cherry trees are coming into flower, and the buds on the trees and bushes grow round and plump until the leaves and shoots inside can contain themselves no longer and burst forth. These are the days that a traveller longs for – the air is warm, the sky is blue and it feels good to be alive.

In the past year we have spent just over four months on the boat, four months house-sitting, and the remainder of the time split between the UK and Le Shack. It has certainly been a year on the move and yet even so I feel as if we are beginning to get into a groove, that there is a danger that we might become set in our ways, particularly if I place it within the context of the last six years. It would be so easy to spend most of our time in France, to fall into a comfortable pattern of long summers on *Olivia Rose* and our winters using house-sits as a base from which to explore new areas. There would be nothing wrong with this, and yet I realise that I don't want to get into a groove, don't want life to become a comfortable, predictable pattern.

We have exciting plans for this coming year, but equally exciting are all the days that don't fall within those plans, days when something unexpected happens, when we are tempted to walk down a different road and see where it leads, for better or for worse. Perhaps I should add this last point to the reasons why travel means so much to me. It's the heady attraction of not knowing what lies ahead, that tingle up the spine as Michael and I look at each other and, hardly needing to say it, know that we're about to stray off the route and that it feels like the right thing to do.

In my first book, *Just Passing Through*, I said that there was something irresistibly romantic about living and travelling on a boat. Six years later those words are truer than ever but now they apply to our whole year, rather than just the summers spent on the water. As constant travellers we never journey alone, although our companions are elusive and fickle at times. Romance is still with us, floating imperceptibly on a summer's breeze, and now she has been joined by mystery, who cloaks himself in the early morning tendrils of fog along the river. Joy lies buried deep in the song of the nightingale and contentment peeks shyly down on us, hiding behind a full moon.

What comes next? I can't answer that question in any detail yet. This book is coming to an end but if the next book were a drawing it would be there in outline only, like one of Michael's sketches when he is playing with shape and shadow. We have to be patient and see how life fills in the empty spaces. The only thing I do know is that we will keep travelling and I hope to welcome you back again in the not too distant future.

❖ ❖ ❖

Please review this book!

Please leave a review – *reviews really matter*. They are what sell books so if you are happy to leave either a written review or an anonymous star rating, I would be hugely grateful.

Acknowledgements

My grateful thanks to the team as always: Louise Lubke Cuss at Wordblink for her copyediting, Georgia Laval at Laval Editing for formatting and Ebook Launch for the cover design. You help to make this book the best it can be. A special mention for Helen Isaacs who is my beta reader, checks my French for me and is always there when I need to brainstorm an idea and calms me down when I want to throw the whole thing in the bin. Thank you also to Tricia Houlton for her feedback on punctuation and spelling. Last but not least of course, a big thanks to my husband Michael for his beautiful drawings and for sharing the journey.

About the author

Mary-Jane lives a nomadic life in Europe with her husband Michael. They have a small off-grid cabin close to the French Pyrenees but spend very little time there, preferring instead to travel on their boat in the summer months and using house-sitting as a cost-effective way to travel and explore new areas over the winter.

She has written four books under the umbrella title of *In Search of a Simple Life*. The first is *Just Passing Through* which follows them in their first three years as they sell their house, buy a boat and learn how to live on the water. The second book, *A Simple Life*, has been an Amazon Bestseller and shares their experiences as fate takes an unexpected turn and they find themselves living in a tiny cabin in the south west of France with no electricity, no kitchen, bedroom or bathroom and where the loo is a bucket in the shed. The third book, *The Turning of the Seasons*, looks back to a more settled time in their lives when they had a smallholding in Wales. This latest book, *The Constant Traveller*, sees them back out on the water once more, and follows them as they fall ever more deeply in love with their nomadic lifestyle.

She has also written *How to be a House-Sitter*: A creative way to stretch the budget for people with a passion for travel.

When asked to describe herself, Mary-Jane says she loves blue skies, new places and new faces. She delights in finding pleasure in the small things and keeping life simple. Forever restless, and always looking around the next corner, she can think of no better life for herself than the one she now lives.

Excerpt from *How to be a House-Sitter*

Have you ever thought of being a house-sitter? If so you might enjoy this extract from Mary-Jane's new book, *How to be a House-Sitter:* **A creative way to stretch the budget for people with a passion for travel.**

Introduction

People with a passion for travel often have to think creatively to realise their dreams. Most of us need to work within a budget, and the amount of time we can spend travelling and the distance we can travel may be dependent upon the money we have available to us. House-sitting offers the gift of a cost-effective way to travel around the world, staying for free in homes that are often luxurious, often in wonderful locations, in exchange for looking after both the home and the animals that come with it. It almost seems too good to be true and indeed there is a compromise to be made on two counts: the first is that in theory you can travel anywhere in the world but in practice it will happen only if someone in that area is looking for a house-sitter at the same time as you want to be there. You might have dreamed of an apartment with a sea view in the south of France, but if nothing is available in that precise location you might have to settle for a rural cottage further inland. More importantly, the second compromise comes from the fact that you will be looking after animals, much-adored pets who will be your responsibility, who need to be walked, fed, kept company and who often can't be left for long periods of time. A house-sitter does not have the same freedoms as the carefree traveller paying for their own accommodation and I hope by the time you get to the end of this book you will see that both an interest in, and a love of, animals is a crucial element. That said, as long as you are aware of those compromises from the beginning and can accept them, there is no doubt that house-sitting offers great opportunities for the cost-conscious traveller. I have been doing it since 2017 and can heartily recommend it.

You may be asking yourself why anyone needs a book to tell them how to be a house-sitter. After all, most of us live in a house and therefore we already know how to do it. This is true, but there are a number of good reasons why this is not enough to guarantee that you will become a successful house-sitter. There is a great deal more to it than just turning up, getting a quick tour of the house and taking the dog out for a walk. In fact, most of the work is done before you even get to that point.

This book aims to take you, step by step, through the whole process, beginning with an overview of how the market works. I have compiled a list of the major house-sitting companies and compared what they offer and how much it costs. I have analysed their portfolios, detailing the number of sits they have in each country to make it easier for you to choose the company that suits you best.

I explain exactly what a house-sitter does and balance this with an insight into what a homeowner is looking for when they browse through the sitter profiles. Guidance is given on how to write a profile that will stand out and win you sits. Another important element is how to manage the sit and how to ensure that you get top quality reviews – vital as this business is built on reputation and there is no room for doing a half-hearted job. Where relevant I provide hints and tips and do my best to answer frequently asked questions, such as how you get that first sit when you have no experience, is age or being single an issue, and whether you can manage without your own transport. I share stories of our own and other people's house-sitting experiences so that you get a sense of how it really feels, the ups and downs of it, the joys and frustrations that are all part of looking after animals.

My husband Michael and I have been house-sitting since 2017, when we sold our house in the UK and began a nomadic life. We spend our summers on our boat in Europe, and our winters using house-sitting as a cost-effective way of allowing us to travel and explore new areas. Our experience, at the time of writing, is centred around Europe and the UK and so we have no personal experience of areas such as the States and Australia, both of which offer plentiful house-sitting opportunities.

However many of the same rules apply, regardless of the country, and animals behave in the same way wherever they live.

My objective in writing this book was to equip you with the necessary tools to enjoy this type of life as much as we do. By the time you read the last page I hope I have given you sufficient information so that you understand how the market works, have recognised what you are hoping to achieve, know that this is right for you and have the confidence and knowledge to begin on a new journey. *Bon voyage!*

Printed in Great Britain
by Amazon

60181795R00150